IQRA' Kindergarten Curriculum

Volume 1:
Islamic History

Tasneema Ghazi
PhD Curriculum, University of Minnesota

IQRA'
International Educational Foundation
Chicago

Part of a Comprehensive and Systematic Program of Islamic Studies

---

Approved by:
Rabita al-Alam al-Islami
Makkah Mukarramah

Editors and Reviewers:
Noura Durkee
M.A. Fine Arts, Stanford University
Shahida Ali Khan
Principal, New Horizon School, California

Artists and Designers
Saba Ghazi
B.A. Fine Arts, University of Illinois
Usama Ghazi
Student, University of Redlands
Mike Rezac
B.A. Fine Arts, University of llinois

Under the Auspices of Educational Program Development Committee:
Dr. M.A.W. Fakhri, Chairman
Br. Fadel Abdullah
Br. Mohammad Nur Abdullah
Dr. Abidullah Ghazi, Secretary
Dr. Tasneema Ghazi
Dr. Mohammad Kishta
Dr. Sulayman Nyang

Acknowledgements:
Iqra' Charitable Society for their support and establishment of the Chair of Curriculum Development

Islamic Society of North America and *International Institute of Islamic Thought* for participation in the evaluation and publication effort.

ISBN # 1-56316-253-9

IQRA's Note

We at IQRA' International Educational Foundation are grateful to Allah (SWT) for enabling us to present the kindergarten curriculum of Islamic Studies.

The present volume of IQRA' Curriculum (Kindergarten Sirah), represents four years of painstaking research, study, writing and field testing by Dr. Tasneema Ghazi, IQRA's Director of Curriculum. She was assisted by our able team members of the Program Development Committee, innumerable educators, teachers, community workers, and concerned parents.

IQRA' is pleased to announce that its plans to develop, field test and publish an integrated curriculum for Islamic schools from preschool to high school within the next five years (by July 1997) are well under way.

The development and production of this curriculum is part of IQRA's vision of a comprehensive system of Islamic education which covers:

1. An integrated curriculum from preschool to high school.

2. A comprehensive program of Islamic Studies at all levels to include ten basic Islamic subjects and to cover graded *textbooks*, *workbooks*, *enrichment literature*, *parents/teachers manual* and *educational aids*.

3. An Open University and Home based education.

In each area Iqra's work is progressing in a planned way and we hope within this decade (before we enter the year 2000) IQRA's vision will become a reality, *InshaAllah*.

This kind of effort needs: i) a commitment to make Islamic education our foremost priority, ii) mobilization of communities' human and financial resources, iii) institutionalization of efforts and iv) coordination with other organizations.

We urge all concerned Muslims and Islamic organizations to cooperate with IQRA' and become an *Ansar* of its Educational Program.

Let us together establish IQRA' International Educational Foundation as the finest institution of Islamic educational research and development. It would be the best gift, we the North American Muslims, can give to our children and to the *Ummah* as a whole.

Dedicated To:

Dr. Abdullah Omar Nassief
Our friend, guide and philosopher
An embodiment of the spirit of early Islam

Who

In response to the basic need of Islamic education
supported IQRA' International Educational Foundation
in the fulfillment of its Educational Vision

Table of Contents

Introduction

KINDERGARTEN PROGRAM
IN
AN ISLAMIC SCHOOL

PHILOSOPHY:

The goal of the Kindergarten Program in an Islamic school is to provide opportunities for an active involvement of children, their parents and teachers in a continual process of education based on the knowledge of the Qur'an and the *Sunnah*. Involvement of Muslim parents in the educational process of their children is specially important due to the many non-Islamic influences of the modern Western culture and environment.

Kindergarten is usually the beginning of formal schooling, even though in many educational systems it is not compulsory for a five years old to attend regular school. When a child enters Kindergarten, both he and his parents begin a far reaching experience. For many children this is the first experience of formal schooling and for many parents this is the first encounter with being separated from their child. Kindergarten teachers and school administrators need to plan on building a relationship of trust and understanding between school and home. Once established, this relationship provides many avenues for coordination and cooperation between these two primary institutions in the life of a child.

The source of every Islamic educational program should be the "Revelation" as opposed to pure "reason", as reason without the light of the Revelation is misguided and limited. The curriculum planners, the administrators, the teachers and the parents of Islamic schools should make continuous efforts to integrate Islamic knowledge , behavior, *Akhlaq* and *Adab* in the daily activities of each classroom . Any objective, content and activity which is in conflict with the clear teachings of the Qur'an and the *Sunnah* has no place in a classroom for Muslim children. Thus, it is important that those who are involved in educating and nurturing our children should have a comprehensive knowledge of the Qur'an and the *Sunnah* and as the models of Islamic behavior and living, practice the teachings in their daily lives.

The goal of the program should be the development of an Islamic personality through inculcation of Islamic values and nurturing of Islamic behavior. Keeping in mind the cognitive, social, motor, emotional and physical characteristics of five and six year olds, the emphasis should be on the development of Islamic concepts and acquisition of Islamic practices. The teachers, administrators and older children should be the role model of Islamic behavior and living for the Kindergartners who learn and adopt new behaviors easily and quickly from those, they idealize. The importance of learning which takes place during the kindergarten years has been best stated by Robert Fulghum in the following words;

All I really need to know I learned in Kindergarten

All I really need to know about how to live and what to do and how to be I learned in Kindergarten. Wisdom was not at the top of the graduate -school mountain, but there in the sandpile at Sunday School. These are the things I learned. Share everything. Play fair. Don't hit people. Put things back where you found them. Clean up your own mess. ....

(Robert Fulghum)

To achieve the goals, the Kindergarten program should provide for the child:

1) Opportunities for physical, social, motor, emotional, cognitive and moral development to the extent of his and her capabilities and the rate of his or her own development.

2) An Islamic environment so that the moral and spiritual I self of the child can develop under the teachings of the Qur'an and the *Sunnah.*

3) A secure and safe environment so that the child will not be afraid to try new experiences.

4) Varied kind of experiences for learning, mastering and completing developmental tasks.

5) Warm and supportive adults to guide and encourage both individual and group activities and to act as suitable Muslim role models for the children.

6) Freedom, opportunities and encouragement towards developing responsibility, self control and independence with respect for others.

7) Loving, clear and meaningful beginning lessons in the teachings of the Qur'an, *Hadith, Sirah,* Islamic *Akhlaq,*Islamic *Fiqh & 'Ibadat* and Islamic history providing a foundation for a lifetime of practice and study.

CHARACTERISTICS OF YOUNG CHILDREN BETWEEN THE AGES OF FIVE AND SIX YEARS

Children between the ages of five and six years are approaching the end of the period of Early Childhood. Following are some of the specific characteristics of five and six year olds.

PHYSICAL:

"A normally active Kindergartner is a busy, curious and industrious child" (Harris et.al, 1986, p. 323). He manages his body movements with more skill and comfort. He can walk backward with toe and heel pattern. Can run fast, skip, hop and play games. He is able to balance on one foot, jump and land on toes, jump down two or three steps.

He can take care of himself by washing without splashing water on his clothes, dressing himself and tying his shoe laces. A Kindergarten child enjoys water play, building with blocks and large boxes , can build three dimensional structures. He can use tools such as scissors, screw drivers and hammer etc, . Working with the puzzles is one of the favorite play for the children between the ages of five and six .

Fine motor coordination develops to a point where he is able to copy triangle and diamond. He can begin to print some letters or numbers and his name correctly. Can draw recognizable life like representations and a definite preference for left or right handedness is established.

VISION:

The five and six year olds can coordinate the senses of touch, hearing and vision almost as well as adults. As opposed to three and four year-olds who rely more on touch while exploring the environment, the five and six year-olds rely more on vision (White et.al, 1964). Thus, while exploring the unfamiliar objects three and four year-olds depend more on the sense of TOUCH, whereas five and six year olds pay more attention to the color and size of the object and use more visual clues.

COGNITIVE:

Children between the ages of five and six years are still at the "pre-operational stage" where symbolic thinking dominates much of their life. Symbolic thinking enables them to have a schema of the words and images represent an object or certain actions in the mind of the child. He is capable of using language more meaningfully.However, this ability of symbolic thinking is accompanied by important characteristics referred by Piaget as "Egocentrism", "Animism" , "Finalism: and "Centration".

Egocentrism is the condition where children think and experience every event in relation to themselves. Even the phenomenon of nature happen because of them as the center, for example the sun rises to make them feel happy and for them to play outside, night falls to make them sleep , Mom and Dad go to work to get money for them to buy things etc.

Animism refers to the child's tendency to attribute life like qualities to inanimate objects for example, attributing pain and happiness to dolls and stuffed animals. However, by the age five and six they begin to move away from this condition and have some idea of the differences between animate and inanimate objects. They still make errors in judgement.

Finalism is the belief of the pre-operational child that every action accomplishes some purposes. The "purposes" attributed to each action is unique to each child. They believe that every movement (by human or an object) is "goal directed" because their own movements are goal directed.

Centration refers to the inclination of the pre-operational child to concentrate only on a single aspect of a situation and neglect all others. They do not understand that a change in the appearance of certain object does not necessarily mean that the object has lost many other of its attributes. For example they believe that a tall slender glass holds more water than a shorter wide glass, even though they both have the capacity of holding the same amount of water.

Concept Formation is one of the most important achievements of early childhood years. "Concepts" according to Piaget, ' are cognitive categories that help children and adults organize information and acquire new knowledge'. Environment provided for the children during these early years helps in the development of specific concept, which makes the role of "important adults" in the life of children significantly important.

LANGUAGE DEVELOPMENT:

Language development takes place at a very fast pace to help the child express his own ideas. The vocabulary grows to 8,000 - 14,000 words by age six. Length of the sentences increases from three words per sentence at age 2-3 to 6-8 words per sentence by the ages five and six years. More "WH' words are used (why, whom, where and when). Children tend to ask more questions.

SOCIAL DEVELOPMENT:

Five and six year-olds develop more social skills which are reflected in their play which becomes more associative and co-operative. They play together to help each other in the achievement of certain goal. There is a tendency to help each other during play and other activities.

Kindergarten children are more ready for a few hours' separation from their parents than the younger children. They are ready to share, be considerate to other, wait for their turn and accept small responsibility (when required to do so) in the classroom. According to Piaget children between the ages of three and five believe that the rules are generated by an external authority such as God, parents or teachers and can not be changed . However, due to egocentrism, they practice their own version of rules, ignoring or changing the existing rules.

EMOTIONAL DEVELOPMENT

The Kindergarten child is still quite egocentric, even though he becomes more considerate of others. Most of the fears of early childhood begin to subside. Five and six year-olds are more willing to accept the reasoning and explanations for the occurrences which frighten them. They tend to pay attention to the causes (given to them) of why and how things happen. In short, they can distinguish between the reality and the fantasy. Anger is expressed more verbally and physically than in the temper tantrums. They are ready to accept and follow the rules.

Teachers and parents should be aware of the feelings and emotions of the children. Adults should be sensitive to the expressed feelings of the children. It is difficult for them at this stage to keep up with their own pace. For example, they strive to do too many things by themselves but when things build up and become too much to handle, the teachers and parents should give a helping hand. The children have to understand that it is okay to be dependent upon someone for a while.

Classroom activities should be planned keeping in mind the above characteristics of the children.

HOW TO USE THE CURRICULUM GUIDE

We have made an attempt to develop a comprehensive and integrated curriculum guide, covering five areas of Islamic education viz:

Teachings of the Qur'an
Sirah of Prophet Muhammad (S)
Aqa'id and *Fiqh*
Islamic History
Islamic *Akhlaq* and *Adab*

The curriculum guide is integrated in the sense that there are constant cross references of goals, objectives and suggested activities from one subject area to the other. A teacher teaching all five subjects to the same grade or level can take advantage of this scheme of integration. However, keeping in mind the needs of the teachers who teach only one subject, the curriculum for each subject at each level is kept quite independent. Following are some special features of this curriculum guide:

Statement of the Philosophy

The Curriculum guide opens with a philosophy statement. We request everyone of you to read the statement and develop a solid and clearly defined philosophical basis for your school and your classroom.

Characteristics of children between the ages of five and six years

Under this heading is a brief description of the physical, cognitive, social and emotional development of Kindergarten age children. We urge you to read it and try to understand the behavior and learning process of children under your supervision while in school. Most of the teachers and parents will need more information about the developmental process of young children than provided here , which can be easily obtained by reading any of the recommended books on Child Development.(See Bibliography).

Scope and Sequencece chart

This chart represents the total sequence of the units to be covered during the course of one academic year of Kindergarten. SCOPE refers to the amount of information which is made available to the children at a particular grade level.

For example the Sequence of "Islamic History " component of the Kindergarten curriculum is from Adam (A) to Prophet Ibrahim (A) . The history of the prophets is introduced in the same chronological order as mentioned in the Qur'an, thus, following five prophets are introduced in the sequence:

Adam (A)---- Nuh (A)----Hud (A) ----- Salih (A) -------and Ibrahim (A)
The next eight will be introduced in the First grade and the rest in the third and fourth grades, *InshaAllah.* The Scope of Islamic history curriculum is determined keeping in mind the physical, cognitive, social and emotional development of children between the ages of five to eight years. Amount of time available to the teacher of Islamic history is also an important contributing factor in determining the Scope.

THE SCHEME

Unit: Total spectrum of selected topics is divided into Units. A Unit represents a topic or an area of study. Each Unit is divided into many Lessons. Each Lesson is developed around one aspect of the Unit. Some units are larger and have more Lessons than others.

Each Unit begins with specific "Learning Experiences and Activities" to be developed through various lessons. Please read them carefully so you are aware of them during your lesson planning and teaching. Following the rules of curriculum integration, "learning experiences" in various areas of learning are imbedded within each Unit.It is suggested that special attention should be paid to these details.

Lesson: Each Lesson cvonsists of:

Focal Point is the theme of the lesson---the goal itself.

Behavioral objectives are the objectives of the lesson stated in measurable behavioral terms. It is hoped that children , after successfully completing the lesson, will be able to demonstrate the desired changes in their daily behavior. Teachers and parents should make sure that the intended behavior is learned and acquired by each child after the completion of each lesson. Mastery of these behavioral Objectives by each child is essential for continuous learning and concept formation.

Suggested Activities are only "suggested" activities to help the teachers plan their lesson. By no means any teacher is bound to use only these activities. We encourage you to be innovative, plan your own activities, use those suggested or even improvise the suggested activities according to your need. No matter what you as the teacher do just remember that you have to have well developed lesson plans before entering the classroom. It is also important to plan some time during the class period for children's participation and interaction . Sometimes the worksheets are provided for the teachers to use in the class.

Evaluation Forms At the end of each Unit, there is an evaluation form, that is for us. We would like you to take some time and complete the form after completing each Unit and mail it to our offices. This is our way of involving you in the process of curriculum development and field testing. Your input as the person in the classroom using the curriculum guide is absolutely essential for the validity of this curriculum. This is the first draft for field testing and evaluation.

Please feel free to get in touch with us at the Iqra' Foundation. We welcome your valuable comments and suggestions

ISLAMIC HISTORY

PHILOSOPHY

وَكُلًّا نَّقُصُّ عَلَيْكَ مِنْ أَنبَاءِ الرُّسُلِ مَا نُثَبِّتُ بِهِۦ فُؤَادَكَ وَجَاءَكَ
فِي هَٰذِهِ الْحَقُّ وَمَوْعِظَةٌ وَذِكْرَىٰ لِلْمُؤْمِنِينَ ﴿١٢٠﴾

All that We relate to thee of the stories of the messengers
with it we make firm thy heart; in them cometh to thee the
Truth, as well an exhortation and a message of remembrance
to those who believe.

(AlHud 11:120)

The history curriculum for an Islamic Kindergarten should attempt to provide experiences in Islamic living through the examples of those Muslims who have lived before us. Life and stories of the Prophets of Allah (SWT) as mentioned in the Qur'an and the *Hadith* are the best medium to introduce Islamic history to young Muslims. We, at the Iqra' Foundation, believe in developing a historical perspective where historical materials are not only used as a static chain of events, dates and names, instead, it becomes a basic source of learning which students can relate to their own life experiences and which can guide them in understanding their environment and in searching for their own place in society. Through studying the attitudes and responses of different people to the messages of the Prophets of Allah (SWT) children should be aided in gaining an insight into the process of the presentation of the message, the process of the resistance and rejection of Truth and its ultimate triumph.

The children should also be made aware of the relationship between the obedience of the followers of the Truth and Allah's rewards for them and the disobedience of people to Allah's commands and His punishment. Gaining insight into these processes will lead children to be receptive to the teachings of the Qur'an and the *Sunnah.* They will be encouraged to adopt the teachings productively in their daily lives at their own level.

The focus of Islamic history program in an Islamic school should be what Allah (SWT) has told us in the Qur'an:

لَقَدْ كَانَ فِي قَصَصِهِمْ عِبْرَةٌ لِّأُولِي الْأَلْبَابِ مَا كَانَ حَدِيثًا يُفْتَرَىٰ وَلَٰكِن تَصْدِيقَ
الَّذِي بَيْنَ يَدَيْهِ وَتَفْصِيلَ كُلِّ شَيْءٍ وَهُدًى وَرَحْمَةً لِّقَوْمٍ يُؤْمِنُونَ ﴿١١١﴾

There is in their stories instruction for men endued with
understanding. It is not a tale invented but a confirmation
Of what went before it. A detailed exposition of all things
And a Guide and a Mercy to those people who believe
(*Surah* Yusuf 12: *Ayah:* 111)

A NOTE TO THE TEACHERS:

It is important to remember that the two very common modern ideas; **progress** and **evolution** are the running theme of almost all science and educational literature. Most of the films children will see, and many books they will read assume biological and social evolution. Remember to point to the children that the first conscious human being Adam (A) knew more than anyone knows today about the truth and reality. Also remind them that the best moral society that ever will be -- existed in Madinah 1400 years ago during the time of Muhammad Rasulullah (S) and the *Khulafa' Ar-Rashidun.* Point out that the best among us are those who obey Allah (SWT) and follow the Qur'an and the *Sunnah* in their daily living .

As Muslims, we must follow the example of the Madinah society in both our personal and community lives. The truth of *Tawhid* and the reality of leading a moral and virtuous life has been a constant theme in human history, explained to us through the examples of the prophets and the teachings of the revelations. Human society has progressed materially, however, it needs a moral foundation to hold itself together. Each human society must understand and implement these messages and the teachings in their social life, so that it is not completely lost in the material pursuits.

Unit One: Prophet Adam (A)

lessons 1-6

UNIT ONE

LEARNING EXPERIENCES AND ACTIVITIES

1. LEARNING CONCEPTS (Moral Perspectives)

Belief in the Prophets of Allah (SWT)
Respect for the Prophets of Allah (SWT)
Understanding that we are all children of Adam (A)
Obedience to Allah (SWT) is rewarded
Disobedience to Allah (SWT) is punished
Repentence of Adam (A) and Hawwa
Forgiveness of Allah (SWT)
Disobedience of Allah (SWT)

2. LEARNING SKILLS

Vocabulary
Comparison
Contrast
Sequencing
Reasoning

3. HISTORICAL PERSPECTIVE

Story of the Creation of Adam (A)
Allah's (SWT) command of all the angels and jinns.
Refusal of Iblees and Allah's (SWT) punishment
Knowledge, Allah's (SWT) gift to Adam (A) and to all of us through him.
Sequence of events which lead to the expulsion of Iblees from Jannah.
Creation of Hawwa (R).
Concept of Jannah, the home of the newly created human couple.
Disobedience of Allah's (SWT) commands by Adam (A) and Hawwa (R).
Allah's (SWT) punishment to the couple and expulsion from Jannah.
Repentence and forgiveness.
Children of Adam (A) and Hawwa (R)

4. GEOGRAPHICAL PERSPECTIVE

Description of Jannah
Fall of Adam (A) and Hawwa (R) from Jannah to Earth.
Areas in the world where children of Adam (A) and Hawwa (R) spread.

5. CIVIC PERSPECTIVE

Adam (A) and Hazrat Hawwa (R) - The finest and superior creation of Allah (SWT)
Responsibilities of human being because of the position.
Concept of equality of human race - everyone is the child of the original couple.

6. LINGUISTIC PERSPECTIVE

Listening
Oral language
Dictating the stories
Re-telling the story
Vocabulary
Sight vocabulary

7. ARTISTIC EXPRESSIONS

Coloring
Pasting
Painting
Drawing
Songs and rhymes

TIME REQUIREMENTS

Time needed: 7-8 class hours (30 min. each)

Sunday school: 8 lessons (30 min. each)

Full time school: 7 lessons (45 min. each)
plus one lesson for evaluation

Proposed References For Teachers of Islamic History

History of the Prophets (S)

Arabic

١- قصص الانبياء \ لابن كثير.

٢- قصص القرآن \ لجاد المولى.

English

Muhajir, Ali Musa Raza — Lessons from the Stories of the Quran, Sh.Muhammad Shraf Publishers

Nadwi, Sayyed Abul Hasan — Stories of the Prophets, UK Islamic Academy

Urdu قصص القران : مولانا حفظ الرحمن سیوہاروی - ندوۃ المصنفین - دہلی

IQRA' KINDERGARTEN CURRICULUM
ISLAMIC HISTORY
UNIT 1: Prophet Adam (A), The First Man
Lesson 1: Creation

FOCAL POINT	PERFORMANCE OBJECTIVES	SUGGESTED ACTIVITIES	RESOURCE MATERIAL
A> Allah (SWT) is the Creator	**The children will:** -know that Allah (SWT) is The Creator	**The teacher will:** **a.** Introduce the lesson by sharing with the children, (in group setting - rugtime), pictures and posters of the Earth, ocean, rivers, landscape and discuss- - What is this? - Who is this? - What is happening here?	Pictures of oceans, trees, Earth, etc.
B> Allah (SWT) has created everything	-learn about the earth -recognize its inhabitants in relation to its geography and terrain -participate in language arts exercises	**a.** Introduce the story (See "A" below) **b.** Use large title labels with the story and point to each word while telling the story to the children. **c.** Retell the story by writing it on the large writing pad. Leave blanks for the children to fill in. Once the story is completed, review these words with the children, by pointing them out. **d.** Make sure that children follow left to right eye movement and direction while reading with you.	Pictures of various animals and humans and nature - OR - have flannel board cut-outs of all these. Flannel board patterns to depict the story.
A> SKILLS Auditory Discrimination	VOCABULARY Message Obedience Punished Pair		

THE STORY OF CREATION AND THE BEGINNING OF MAN

Allah (SWT) created the stars, the sun, the moon, and all the other planets. Allah (SWT) also created the Earth. On the Earth, he created all the oceans, forests, mountains, rivers, trees, and flowers. Then, Allah (SWT) wanted to create a man, and so He did. He called the man **Adam** -- the first man ever. Adam (A) was a very special creation of Allah (SWT). Allah (SWT) gave him special knowledge of things. He gave him a mind to think and choose with. He gave him a heart to feel and love with. Allah (SWT) asked Adam (A) to live in a special place called the **Jannah**. Jannah means "garden". Allah (SWT) gave everything to Adam (A). He was very happy in the Jannah. Allah (SWT) made Adam (A) His first prophet.

MANY CREATIONS OF ALLAH (SWT)

HE ALSO CREATED

HE ALSO CREATED

HE ALSO CREATED

NOTE: *Let the children draw the pictures of His creations (e.g. trees, flowers, the sun, mountains, etc.)*

IQRA' KINDERGARTEN CURRICULUM

ISLAMIC HISTORY

UNIT 1: Prophet Adam (A), The First Man

Lesson 2: The First Man

FOCAL POINT	PERFORMANCE OBJECTIVES	SUGGESTED ACTIVITIES	RESOURCE MATERIAL
A> Reading, Writing, Vocabulary	**The children will:** -learn new vocabulary -develop language arts skills	**The teacher will:** **a.** Teach new vocabulary words in the context of the stories being studied. For example, give the students several pictures and clues and ask them to find a picture from those provided.	Scissors, Glue, Magazine Pictures, etc.
B> Comprehension	-learn that Allah (SWT) is The Creator of everything	**a.** Carry out exercises to enhance the literal, inferential and critical comprehension of the lesson. Below are some examples: -Make a worksheet to check literal comprehension (see A below). -Ask comprehension questions. -Ask the children to give a general description of the Jannah. (e.g. It is beautiful. It is peaceful.)	
C> Reasoning	-learn about the Jannah	**a.** Ask the children to describe what they think the Jannah will be like.	Pens and Paper

IQRA' KINDERGARTEN CURRICULUM
ISLAMIC HISTORY
UNIT 1: Prophet Adam (A), The First Man
Lesson 2: The First Man
continued . . .

FOCAL POINT	PERFORMANCE OBJECTIVES	SUGGESTED ACTIVITIES	RESOURCE MATERIAL
D> Cause and Effect	-learn that Adam (A) was the first man created by Allah (SWT), and we are here today because we are his children.	**a.** Help the children understand the concept that Allah (SWT) has created all creatures large and small by examples, going from big to small. For example have the children look at a bug, a tiny bird, a small cat etc. up to an elephant and each time ask, "Who created it?" **b.** Do the same as in **(a)** above, but this time go from large to small. Then have the children stand up, and ask them, "Who created him? Who created her?" Then have the children point to parts of their bodies and ask, "Who created this (head, arm, etc.)?" Then point to smaller parts, such as hands and toes, and then even smaller parts such as fingernails and teeth, then even smaller parts like strands of hair or the pupil of the eye, and ask again, "Who created all of these?" **c.** Have the children listen to their hearts and breath and stomachs, and ask them, "Who made all of this work? Are you doing it yourselves? Who is helping you to be alive?"	Markers, Crayons

COMPREHENSION QUIZ

Procedure: Color every thing created by Allah (SWT).

Now, color the others!

IQRA' KINDERGARTEN CURRICULUM
ISLAMIC HISTORY
Unit 1: Prophet Adam (A), the First Man
Lesson 2: The First Man
Worksheet A: Comprehension Quiz

2. Name of the very first man Allah (SWT) created begins with the letter . . .

B C M A D S

3. Allah (SWT) gave Adam (A) a ________________ to love with.

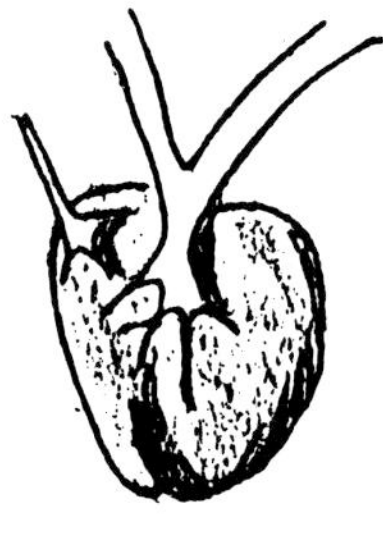

HEART

EYE

EAR

4. Allah (SWT) gave Adam (A) a ________________ to think with.

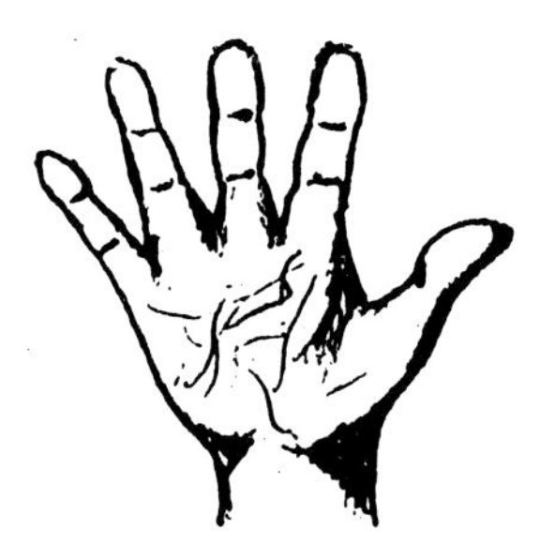

HAND

MOUTH

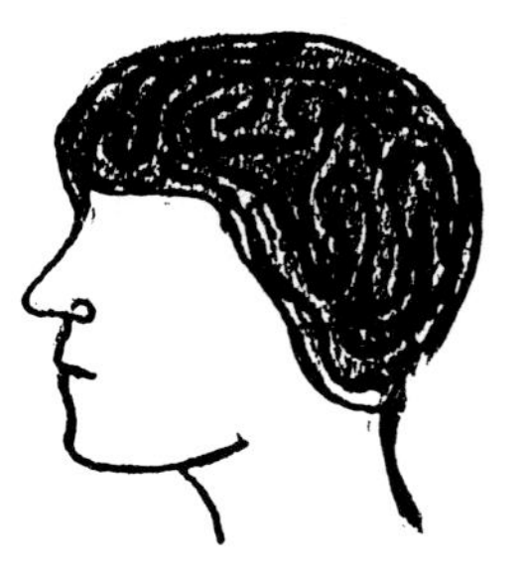

BRAIN

IQRA' KINDERGARTEN CURRICULUM

ISLAMIC HISTORY

UNIT 1: Prophet Adam (A),The First Man

Lesson 3: Iblees and his Disobedience to Allah (SWT)

FOCAL POINT	PERFORMANCE OBJECTIVES	SUGGESTED ACTIVITIES	RESOURCE MATERIAL
A> Disobedience to Allah's commands causes His anger and possible punishment.	The children will: -learn that Iblees refused to obey Allah and bow in front of Prophet Adam (A).	The teacher will: **a.** Read to the children Episode 2 of The Story of Adam. (See A below.) **b.** Make flannel board cut-outs and tell the story. (See B below for cut-out patterns.) **c.** Ask the children to retell the story and then write it on the large writing pad. Read the dictated story and then display it on the wall along with the first part of the story. (Language experience) **d.** Play the word association game. (See C below.)	The Story of Adam: Episode 2 Flannel board and cut-outs Markers and Poster board Pens and Paper
B> Moral and religious values and the concept of right and wrong	-learn to differentiate between obedience and disobedience	**a.** Carry out simple analogy and contrasting exercises related to the story of Adam (A). Be sure to emphasize the fact that the angels couldn't think as Adam did. They can think but they have no choice. Allah didn't teach them what He taught Adam (A).	Worksheet

this lesson continues on the next page

IQRA' KINDERGARTEN CURRICULUM

ISLAMIC STUDIES

UNIT 1: Prophet Adam (A),The First Man

Lesson 3: Iblees and his Disobedience to Allah (SWT)
continued . . .

FOCAL POINT	PERFORMANCE OBJECTIVES	SUGGESTED ACTIVITIES	RESOURCE MATERIAL
C> Belief in the angels and jinns as special creations of Allah (SWT)	-learn that Allah (SWT) created the angels -learn that angels are created to worship Allah (SWT) and obey His commands -learn that jinns are also created by Allah (SWT). Iblees was a special jinn who disobeyed Allah's command -develop vocabulary skills (special, creation, bow, disobedience.)	**a.** Relate the lesson in Fiqh on basic beliefs of a Muslim and especially basic belief in angels. **b.** Incorporate the revelations of the Qur'an to Rasulullah (S) through the Angel Jibril (R) from the lessons in Sirah. **c.** Relate how Allah gave Adam (A) knowledge of many things which the angels and the jinns didn't know, discuss with the children and allow them to be imaginative and creative. **d.** Use the vocabulary words enough times, and in various sentences so that the children will develop an understanding for the words.	Fiqh "Our Prophet" Part I Iqra' Foundation

THE DISOBEDIENCE OF IBLEES

Allah (SWT) taught Adam (A) many things. He taught him the names of things He gave Adam (A) special knowledge. The angels did not know as much as Adam (A) did. Allah (SWT) made him very smart. He was a very special creation of Allah (SWT).

Then one day, Allah (SWT) asked the angels and the jinns to come and see Adam (A), His new creation. When everyone gathered, Allah (SWT) asked the angels to tell Him the names of some things. But, the angels could not answer the questions. They said, "O Allah (SWT), we know only what you have taught us. We do not know the names of these things."

Then, Allah (SWT) asked Adam (A) to give him the names of the same things. Adam (A) was able to give the names, because Allah (SWT) had given him special knowledge and taught him the names of everything.

Allah (SWT) told the angels to bow in front of Adam (A) and told them he was a superior creation. All the angels bowed in front of Adam (A). There was a jinn who was with the angels. His name was Iblees. Iblees was very proud and stubborn. He thought he was better than everyone else, so he decided he wouldn't listen to Allah (SWT). He refused to bow in front of Adam (A). He said, "I am better than him!"

Allah (SWT) is kind and merciful, but he does not like disobedience. Allah (SWT) did not like Iblees' refusal. Allah (SWT) made Iblees leave Jannah forever. Iblees had no choice but to leave Jannah. When he left, he promised to Allah (SWT) that he would try to make Adam (A) and all people after him disobey Allah (SWT). Allah (SWT) gave him permission to try. Allah said that the good people of Allah would never listen to him.

FLANNEL CUT-OUTS

Objectives:

1. word association
2. visual discrimination

Materials Needed:

- felt
- scissors
- magazines with various color pictures

Procedure:

- Using felt, cut out the letters to make the following words:

ALLAH
ADAM (A)
IBLEES
ANGELS
JANNAH

- Cut-out pictures for the things whose names Adam (A) knew, such as trees, flowers, animals, etc. (Let the children's imagination work.)

- In a group situation help and encourage the children to retell the story of Prophet Adam (A) with the help of the flannel board and cut-outs

WORD ASSOCIATION GAME

This is a good way to develop vocabulary and enhance imagination and reasoning. In a group setting, ask children to close their eyes and listen to the stimulus word given by the teacher, think for a minute and say the words which come to mind. The teacher writes the words down as children dictate them. Give the words one by one.

Write the words the children give in response to the stimulus word. For example, "Jannah" as the stimulus word may bring the response "is cool", "peaceful", "fun", etc.

Some possible stimulus words are:

- Jannah
- Earth
- Iblees
- Adam (A)
- Angels

UNIT 1: PROPHET ADAM (A): THE FIRST MAN

Lesson 4: Adam (A) Feels Lonely in Jannah

FOCAL POINT	PERFORMANCE OBJECTIVES	SUGGESTED ACTIVITIES	RESOURCE MATERIAL
A> Human beings need companions (empathy)	**The children will:** -learn that Adam (A) was lonely in Jannah because he was the only human being there.	**The teacher will:** **a.** Introduce the lesson by talking about being home alone. **b.** Discuss children's feelings of loneliness - allowing them to express themselves. **c.** Relate their experiences and feelings to the feelings of loneliness of Adam (A) in Jannah. (Teacher write language experience stories told by the children.)	
B> Allah (SWT) is Kind and Understanding	-learn that after Adam (A), Allah (SWT) created Hawwa (R), the first woman	**a.** Tell the story of the creation of Hazrat Hawwa by Allah (SWT). (See"A" below.)	
C> Allah (SWT) has created men and women to live in peace and share and care for each other	-learn that we as Muslims, are supposed to share what we have.	**a.** Ask the students the ways in which they share what they have.	

ADAM (A), HAWWA (R), AND THE FORBIDDEN FRUIT

Allah (SWT) created all creatures on Earth in pairs. Allah (SWT) created another human being after Adam (A). This human being was a woman named Hawwa (R). She was a beautiful woman. She was a noble woman. Adam (A) and Hawwa (R) lived in Jannah. The Jannah was their home. They were happy there. Allah (SWT) gave them anything they wanted in the Jannah.

Allah (SWT) told Adam (A) and Hawwa (R) to eat from all the fruits and vegetables in Heaven, **except** for the fruits from one tree. Adam (A) and Hawwa (R) were very careful to keep away from this forbidden tree because they wanted to obey Allah (SWT).

However, Iblees did not like Adam (A) and Hawwa (R). Iblees thought it was Adam's fault that Allah had sent him away. He wanted to get Adam and Hawwa kicked out of Heaven. He kept telling them to disobey Allah (SWT). He told them that if they ate the fruit of the forbidden tree, they would live forever Finally one day, Adam (A) and Hawwa (R) both felt like eating the fruit. They Disobeyed Allah's commands and ate the forbidden fruit together.

As soon as they tasted it, they both felt very bad and sorry for listening to Iblees. They tried to hide in the woods and cover themselves. They were ashamed for Allah to see them after what they had done. Allah (SWT) knew what they had done. He ordered them both to leave the Jannah. The Jannah is only for those who obey Allah (SWT). Allah (SWT) sent Adam (A) and Hawwa (R) down to Earth. They were all responsible for their actions against Allah's orders. Adam (A) and Hawwa (R) were both very sad to leave the Jannah. They missed their home there. They both felt very sorry about their sin. Sin means doing something Allah (SWT) does not want us to do.

Adam (A) cried and begged Allah (SWT) for forgiveness. Hawwa (R) also cried and begged for forgiveness. They both asked for Allah's forgiveness day and night. Allah (SWT) is kind and compassionate. He is merciful and just. He believed that Adam (A) and Hawwa (R) were really sorry for their sins. Allah (SWT) knew they would never disobey Him again. He forgave their sins. Adam (A) and Hawwa (R) thanked Him for His kindness. They promised Allah (SWT) they would follow all His commands. Allah (SWT) made Adam (A) his first prophet on Earth. He promised to guide him and those after him, so that those who followed the guidance could return to the Jannah after their life here on Earth.

Iblees remained their enemy. He and his relations are our enemies. Anyone who urges us to disobey Allah (SWT) is a friend of Iblees and we must never listen to him. Iblees always tries to keep us away from the Jannah and his promises are never true.

IQRA' KINDERGARTEN CURRICULUM
ISLAMIC HISTORY
UNIT 1: Prophet Adam (A), The First Man
Lesson 5: Disobedience of Adam (A) and Hawwa (R)

FOCAL POINT	PERFORMANCE OBJECTIVES	SUGGESTED ACTIVITIES	RESOURCE MATERIAL
A> Iblees is an enemy of human beings	**The children will:** -learn that Iblees encouraged Adam (A) and Hawwa (R) to disobey Allah (SWT)	**The teacher will:** **a.** Continue to tell the story of Adam (A) and Hawwa (R) during a group setting or during rugtime.	The Story of Adam (A) Quran (2: 30-39) (22: 115-124) (7: 19-27)
B> Obedience to Allah (SWT) is mandatory	-understand that Adam (A) and Hawwa (R) were punished because they did not obey Allah (SWT)	**a.** Discuss the moral implications of obeying Allah, one's parents, and one's teachers.	
C> Disobedience to Allah (SWT) is punished	-learn that breaking laws and rules results in punishment	**a.** Read the stories 1. Pinocchio 2. The story of Pharao and army drowning when chasing Musa (A) to the children at different times to convey the message that disregard for laws is punishable.	The Storybook
D> Mistakes can and should be corrected	-learn the story of Adam (A) and Hawwa's (R) sin, and their repentence	**a.** Tell the story of Adam (A) and Hawwa (R) and their sin. **b.** Tell of their woe and sorrow of doing wrong, and emphasize the fact that they repented.	
E> Allah (SWT) is forgiving and merciful	-learn and believe in Allah's (SWT) great power to forgive	**a.** Discuss how Allah forgave both Adam (A) and Hawwa (R), even though they did not obey his command. Talk of how this shows Allah's great mercy and compassion.	

IQRA' KINDERGARTEN CURRICULUM
ISLAMIC HISTORY
UNIT 1: PROPHET ADAM (A):THE FIRST MAN
Lesson 5: Disobedience of Adam (A) and Hawwa
continued . . .

FOCAL POINT	PERFORMANCE OBJECTIVES	SUGGESTED ACTIVITIES	RESOURCE MATERIAL
F> We should be forgiving	-understand that we as humans should also be forgiving	**a.** Discuss how sometimes we make mistakes and our parents and teachers forgive us. **b.** Tell the students that they should also be forgiving. The teacher should then ask the children to talk about times when they have forgiven someone or when someone else has forgiven them. **c.** Write down these language experiences on the large writing pads, as the children dictate them.	Markers, crayons, large writing pad

IQRA' KINDERGARTEN CURRICULUM
ISLAMIC HISTORY
UNIT 1: PROPHET ADAM (A): THE FIRST MAN
Lesson 6: The Children of Adam (A) and Hawwa (R)

FOCAL POINT	PERFORMANCE OBJECTIVES	SUGGESTED ACTIVITIES	RESOURCE MATERIAL
A> Allah (SWT) is the Provider	**The children will:** -believe that Allah (SWT) is forgiving	**The Teacher will:** **a.** Read (or tell) the story of Adam (A) and Hawwa (R) to the children. (See A below)	Story of Adam (A)
B> Every human being is a descendant of Adam (A) and Hawwa(R)	-learn that Allah (SWT) blessed Adam (A) and Hawwa (R) with many children.	**a.** Make a mural of the continents entitled "Children of Adam (A) and Hawwa (R) - One Big Family" (See "B" below). Point out children of the world (African, European, Asian, Australian, etc.)	Paper Dolls. Pins, Paper, Clothes for Dolls, Scissors, Glue
C> Directions: North, South, East and West	-learn the directions on the map of the world	**a.** Spread a world map and mark the directions of North, South, East and West. **b.** Discuss the names of some of the countries which fall in each one of these directions, especially the countries children in the class have association. **c.** Send a progress report home to the parents. (See C below)	Map of the world, Markers, Crayons, Paper, Scissors, Glue

WE ARE THE CHILDREN OF ADAM (A) AND HAWWA (R)

Adam (A) and Hawwa (R) lived on Earth for a long time. They were the first people on Earth. Allah (SWT) gave them both many children. These children had many children, who had many grandchildren. The children and grandchildren of Adam (A) and Hawwa (R) started to move around the world. They moved to the north, they moved to the south, they moved to the east, they moved to the west.

All of us are the children of Adam (A) and Hawwa (R). This means we are all brothers and sisters. The whole world is one big family and that is why we should try to live in peace and harmony... just like a family.

IQRA' KINDERGARTEN CURRICULUM
ISLAMIC HISTORY
Unit 1: Adam (A), The First Man
Lesson 6: The Children of Adam (A) and Hawwa (R)
Worksheet B: Wall Mural

WALL MURAL: "CHILDREN OF ADAM (A) AND HAWWA (R)"

Objectives:

1. Conceptual development. Belonging to one family human race.
2. Allah (SWT) is the Creator and the Lord of everyone.
3. Introduction to the people of different lands, speaking different languages, having different culture yet being one as children of Adam (A) and his wife.
4. Historical Perspective - concept of passage of time.
5. Geographical perspective

Materials needed:

- map of the world (OHT, OHP)
- butcher paper (one roll)
- tissue paper (all colors)
- scissors
- markers
- glue sticks
- pieces of foil and colored paper
- paper plates
- scissors
- pictures of men, women and children of different racial and cultural origins in their costumes.

Procedure:

1. Cut butcher paper about three yards (or as long as your wall spaces allow you to do).
2. Tape the paper on the wall.
3. Draw OHT world map on to the butcher paper, using a permanent black marker.
4. Cover the entire paper with the map of the world.
5. Spread the paper on the floor or a large table, where it can be kept safe to work on for a few days.
6. Using paper plates and/or construction paper cut human figures of people of different nationalities.
7. Work on one or two nations (or geographical areas) each day with the children.
8. Using the cut up pieces of tissue paper dress the people. (You can use yarn for the hair). Do not be too rigid about the national dress; let the children invent too.
9. Use green and blue tissue paper and gold and silver foil to make the sun, water and the grass on the map.

IQRA' KINDERGARTEN CURRICULUM
ISLAMIC HISTORY
Unit 1: Prophet Adam (A), The First Man
Lesson 6: The Children of Adam (A) and Hawwa (R)
Worksheet C: Progress Report

PROGRESS REPORT

Dear Parents,

Assalam-u 'Alaikum,

Good Very Good Excellent

This is how I would describe the work your child, ______________________, has done on this unit, which deals with Prophet Adam (A) and the creation of the world. Some of the objectives of the unit have been:

1) To develop an understanding that Allah (SWT) is the Only Creator.

2) To help children develop an understanding of the rewards of obedience to Allah (SWT)

3) To help children realize that disobedience to Allah's commands can result in punishment.

4) To help children see the cause and effect relationship between obedience and reward and disobedience and punishment.

5) To make children aware of the story of creation as related in the Qur'an.

6) To enhance children's oral communication skills and widen their vocabulary.

Please help your child at home by talking about the story of the creation as narrated in the Qur'an.

Signed,

____
Kindergarten teacher

Unit Two: Prophet Nuh (A)

lessons 1-3

UNIT TWO

LEARNING EXPERIENCES AND ACTIVITIES

1. LEARNING CONCEPTS (Moral Perspectives)

Belief that Allah (SWT) has sent many Prophets to teach the children of Adam (A) and Hazrat Hawwa right ways.
Respect for all the Prophets of Allah (SWT).
Belief that Nuh (A) was a Prophet of Allah (SWT) because Allah told us this in the Qur'an.
Belief in the teachings of Nuh (A).
Allah protects those who follow His teachings - Allah is merciful.
Disobedience to the teachings of Allah's Prophets can be punished by Him.
Nuh (A) and his people were the children of Adam (A) and Hazrat Hawwa (R).

2. LEARNING SKILLS

Vocabulary (oral)
comprehension
listening
sequencing
reasoning
drawing conclusions

3. HISTORICAL PERSPECTIVE

Story of the Prophet Nuh (A) and his people, who forgot Allah (SWT).
A sense of the timeline in the lives of the Prophets of Allah (SWT). The knowledge and understanding that Prophet Nuh (A) came to earth after Prophet Adam (A), the concept of "before" and "after.
When the leaders of a people disobey the prophets of Allah, the people are also punished along with the leaders.
We should elect God fearing leaders
Allah tells us to learn from the mistakes of people who came before us.
As Muslims we believe in Nuh (A) and his teachings.

4. GEOGRAPHICAL PERSPECTIVE

Location of the land of Nuh (A).
The area of the Great Flood.
Iraq, the country where the Ark came ashore.
Jodi mountain.
Map reading, the direction of Jodi mountain from the country where children are located.
Map reading, directions, North, South, East and West.

5. CIVIC PERSPECTIVE

Laws are for everyone to follow.
Laws are for everyone's benefit.

Allah's laws are for everyone, everywhere and for all the time to come.
Those who break the laws should be punished, even if they are very dear relatives of the judge.
If a lot of people around you are breaking the law. it doesn't justify your doing so - right is right no matter how many people are doing wrong.

6. LINGUISTIC PERSPECTIVE

Listening
Re-telling the story
Comprehension
Vocabulary
Sequencing
Reasoning
Rhyming (songs, finger play)

7. ARTISTIC EXPRESSIONS

Painting
Pasting
Collage
Coloring
Singing and finger play
Draw and play

BIBLIOGRAPHY FOR THE TEACHERS

1. Stories of the Qur'an
2. Stories of the Prophets
3. Qur'an ul-Karim

TIME REQUIREMENTS:

Full time school: 4 class hours (30 minutes each)
3 class hours (30 minutes each during Art period)

Sunday school: 3 class hours (45 minutes each)

(children will need extra out of class time to do the wall mural.)

IQRA' KINDERGARTEN CURRICULUM

ISLAMIC HISTORY

UNIT 2: PROPHET NUH (A)

Lesson 1: Nuh (A), A Prophet of Allah (SWT)

FOCAL POINT	PERFORMANCE OBJECTIVES	SUGGESTED ACTIVITIES	RESOURCE MATERIAL
A> Prophethood	**The children will:** -learn that Nuh (A) was a prophet of Allah (SWT)	**The teacher will:** **a.** Tell the children the story of Prophet Nuh (A). (See A below)	Storybook with the story of Nuh (A)
B> The mission of a prophet	-cut out a pair of animals, and then paste the pair on the ark. -know the names of different animals. -recognize and read the names of the animals	**a.** Make a large wall mural of Prophet Nuh's (A) ark. (See B below) **b.** Sing the song "Noah and His Ark" (See C below)	Paper, Scissors, Markers, Paste.

PROPHET NUH (A) AND THE FLOOD

Nuh (A) was a prophet of Allah (SWT). He was sent to teach the people of his time to follow Allah (SWT). Nuh (A) was a very noble man. He always helped other people. He always told the truth. He did not argue and get into fights with anyone. He was very patient. Nuh (A) lived for a very long time. People in his time had very long lives. His father's name was Malek. Malek loved Nuh (A) very much.

The people in Prophet Nuh's (A) time forgot the teachings of Adam (A). They forgot that Allah (SWT) is the only creator. They forgot that Allah (SWT) is the only God. The people started to worship idols. They used to tell lies, and fight and steal from each other.

Allah asked Prophet Nuh (A) to teach his people. Allah told Nuh (A) to tell the people that:

-They should worship only Allah (SWT)

-They should live in peace

-Everyone should help each other and share whatever they have

-They should be kind to each other, especially to women and children.

Nuh (A) went to his people and told them that he was a prophet of Allah. He gave them Allah's message. However, the people were rude and did not listen to him. They made fun of him. They laughed at him and hurt him. They did not believe Nuh (A). They refused to believe in Allah (SWT). Nuh (A) kept on trying to make them believe in Allah, but the people became worse and worse to him. Nuh (A) prayed to Allah about his people. At last Allah (SWT) told him there was no hope for those who refused to understand. Allah (SWT) was angry with the people. He was going to punish them.

He asked Nuh (A) to build an ark. Nuh (A) gathered the wood he would need. He picked up his tools and started to build the ark, as Allah (SWT) had asked him to do. A few of the people had listened to Prophet Nuh (A). They were his followers and helpers, and they believed in and loved Allah (SWT). They came and helped him build the ark.

When the people saw that Nuh (A) was building a huge ark in the middle of land, they started to make fun of him. They said, "Why are you building an ark when there is no water nearby?!!"

Prophet Nuh (A) always answered, "Allah has asked me to build the ark." The people laughed at him and called him crazy. It took Nuh (A) and his companions a long time to build the ark. They worked every day and night .

Finally, when it was ready, Allah asked Nuh (A) to get a pair of each living animal on board, and so he did.

On came a pair of horses
On came a pair of giraffes
On came a pair of camels
On came a pair of chickens
On came pairs of all kinds of animals, birds and insects.

After all the animals were on board, Nuh (A) started telling the people to come on board, warning them that a big flood was coming, and they would drown. Those who were good and Muslim believed what he said, and got on board. However, those who were not Muslims, did not believe Nuh (A) about the flood. They stayed behind and did not get into the ark. They thought Nuh (A) was telling a lie. Even Prophet Nuh's (A) own wife and one of his sons did not believe him. They refused to believe in Allah. Nuh (A) loved his son very much. When Nuh (A) asked his son to get in the ark he refused and said, "I'll climb up the mountain and be saved from the flood."

Nuh (A) knew that his son would not be safe unless he got in the ark, and he wanted to save him. He asked for Allah's help to make his son believe in Islam and come in the ark. Allah told Nuh (A) that those who do not listen to Allah and His prophets are punished, so his son would be punished.

Nuh (A) closed the doors of the ark. Soon, clouds covered the sky, and it began to rain. It poured and poured for days and nights. Water even started to spring up from the ground in springs and fountains. Everything drowned. All the people drowned. Nuh's (A) son ran to the top of a mountain to escape from the rising water. However, as the rain poured down, even the mountains were covered, and so he also drowned. When Allah (SWT) becomes angry at people, he can punish them.

No one can save anybody from Allah's (SWT) punishment. Allah (SWT) does not like to punish people, except for those who make fun of and attack His prophets and those who do not listen to His commands.

Nuh (A) and all the people who listened to his teachings sailed away with the animals. Finally Allah made the rain stop and the clouds clear. Allah (SWT) made the flood water go back down. The ark came to rest at a spot called Jodi mountain. This mountain is in Iraq. Nuh (A) led the people out of the ark. Everyone prayed to Allah (SWT) and thanked Him for His kindness.

Allah (SWT) saved Nuh (A) and the believers. After the Great Flood, there was not even one disbeliever left on the Earth. As for Nuh (A) and his followers, they lived happily in their new home. Nuh (A) had other sons. They went north, south, east and west. They and their families repopulated the Earth.

Wall Mural of Nuh's (A) Ark

Objectives:

1. To help children develop the concept of Allah's mercy to the believers.
2. To help the children know and believe that Allah (SWT) can help us, even when everyone else thinks it's possible.
3. To help children develop an awareness that nothing and no one can save us from Allah's punishment.
4. Learning the names of animal pairs.
5. Artistic expressions and creativity.
6. Working cooperatively in a group.
7. Following directions.

Materials needed:

- butcher paper
- construction paper of different colors
- glue
- paste
- scissors
- markers
- stapler
- tissue
- masking tape

Procedure:

- On a large piece of butcher paper, draw a large Ark.
- Cut the ark in the shape.
- On the construction paper trace the pictures of animals in pairs.
- Ask each child to cut the picture from the construction paper
- Write the name of each animal pair (male and female) on the picture with the children. If they recognize the animal (as you show it to them), write the name on the picture in big letters.
- With the help of the children, paste/staple the pair of animals on to the ark.
- Display the completed mural on the wall.

NOAH AND HIS ARK

The Lord told Noah there's going to be a floody, floody;
Lord told Noah there's going to be a floody, floody;
Made those people feel so muddy, muddy;
Muslims all over the world.
So rise'n shine and give God your glory, glory;
Rise'n shine and give God your glory, glory;
Rise'n shine and give God your glory, glory;
Muslims all over the world.

The animals they came, they came in twosies, twosies;
Animals they came, they came in twosies, twosies;
Elephants and Kangaroosies, roosies;
Muslims all over the world.
So rise'n shine and give God your glory, glory;
Rise'n shine and give God your glory, glory;
Rise'n shine and give God your glory, glory;
Muslims all over the world.

It rained and poured for forty daisies, daisies;
Rained and poured for forty daisies, daisies;
Made those people feel so crazy, crazy;
Muslims all over the world
So rise'n shine and give God your glory, glory;
Rise'n shine and give God your glory, glory;
Rise'n shine and give God your glory, glory;
Muslims all over the world.

The sun came up and dried up the landy, landy;
Sun came up and dried up the landy, landy;
Made those people feel so dandy, dandy;
Muslims all over the world.
So rise'n shine and give God your glory, glory;
Rise'n shine and give God your glory, glory;
Muslims all over the world.

IQRA' KINDERGARTEN CURRICULUM
ISLAMIC HISTORY
UNIT 2: PROPHET NUH (A)
Lesson 2: Allah's (SWT) Punishment for Disobedient People

FOCAL POINT	PERFORMANCE OBJECTIVES	SUGGESTED ACTIVITIES	RESOURCE MATERIAL
A> The prophet's mission	**The children will:** -learn that Nuh (A) was sent by Allah to teach his people. -learn that many of his people did not listen to his teachings	**The teacher will:** **a.** After reading the story to the children, ask the children comprehension questions. -What is the name of the second prophet who came after Adam (A)? (literal) -What did Nuh (A) teach his people? (literal) -What did his people tell him? (inferential/literal) -Why did the people not listen to Nuh (A)? (inferential) -Whose message was Nuh (A) giving to people?	
B> Allah (SWT) can become angry with those who do not listen to His messengers and their teachings.	-learn that Allah is kind and merciful, but He can become angry at us -learn that disobedience to Allah is punished. -do things to please Allah and stay away from whatever displeases Him	**a.** Continue with questions. -When the people did not obey Nuh (A), who were they really disobeying? (Reasoning) -What happened to the people who disobeyed Allah? (critical) -Before Prophet Nuh (A), who else was punished for disobeying Allah? [Adam (A) and Hawwa (R)] -If Prophet Nuh (A) came today, do you think people would listen to him. Would you listen to him? How does Allah (SWT) speak to us today? **b.** Discuss the lesson in such a way that the system of cause (disobedience to Allah) and effect (punishment by Allah) is illustrated. **c.** Discuss what happened to the people who listened to Nuh (A) and obeyed Allah.	
C> SKILLS Auditory discrimination	VOCABULARY Message Obedience Punished Pair		

IQRA' KINDERGARTEN CURRICULUM

ISLAMIC HISTORY

UNIT 2: PROPHET NUH (A)

Lesson 3: We Are Muslims, We Follow Allah's (SWT) Command

FOCAL POINT	PERFORMANCE OBJECTIVES	SUGGESTED ACTIVITIES	RESOURCE MATERIAL
A> Obedience to Allah and his prophets	**The children will:** -Learn the cause and effect relationship between disobedience to Allah (SWT) and punishment from Him.	**The teacher will:** **a.** Discuss the meaning of the words FLOOD and ARK. **b.** Help the children make different kinds of boats and ships etc. **c.** Encourage oral language. Teachers and adults working with the children should have channels of communication open all the time, by talking, interacting, and listening to the children, thereby nurturing into them a habit of listening with attention. **d.** Carry out language experience exercises, by having the children tell the story, and then writing it on the large writing pad, while the children dictate. **e.** Make a book on Prophet Nuh's (A) story, dictated and illustrated by the children. Talk about how the animals were obedient to Allah (SWT) and came from all over to be in the ark. Show pictures of animals so the children will understand the situation of having all those different animals in the ark (sound, cages, food, etc.)	 Papers, Glue, Paste Marker and Large Writing pad
B> <u>SKILLS</u> Recall and Recognition	<u>VOCABULARY</u> Ark Flood Noble Patience Idols Message Names of the animals	**a.** Send a progress report home to the parents of the children. (See <u>A</u> below)	

PROGRESS REPORT

Dear Parents,

Assalam - u ' Alaikum

GOOD VERY GOOD EXCELLENT

That is how I describe the work that your child, ____________________, has done on this unit, which dealt with Prophet Nuh (A). Some of the objectives of this unit have been:

1) To build your child's faith in the mission of the prophets of Allah (SWT).

2) To give your child a sense of Islamic history at his/her own level.

3) To develop Iman in your child and instil in him/her an understanding of the virtues of obeying Allah's commandments.

4) To help your child understand the basic causal relationship between obedience and reward, and disobedience and punishment from Allah (SWT).

5) To develop and enhance his/her skills in the field of oral communication, reading, and vocabulary.

Thank You very much for taking the time to read this letter. May the peace and blessings of Allah (SWT) be upon you.

Signed,

____
Kindergarten teacher

Unit Three: Prophet Hud (A)

lessons 1-3

UNIT THREE

LEARNING EXPERIENCES AND ACTIVITIES

1: LEARNING CONCEPTS (MORAL PERSPECTIVES)

Respect for the prophets of Allah (SWT)
Allah has sent prophets to many people in the world at different times
Allah loves those who prays and do good deeds
Denial of Allah is punished
The love of the prophets for their people

2: LEARNING SKILLS

Vocabulary
Comparison
Evaluation
Drawing Conclusions
Sequencing
Reasoning

3: HISTORICAL PERSPECTIVE

The name of Prophet Hud's (A) people - Aad
The valley of Al-Ahkaf
Prophet Hud (A) was a descendant of Prophet Muhammad (S)
Aad's great architects and craftsmen
The story of Hud (A) and his teachings
Allah's punishment to the people of Aad
Allah favors those who listen to Him and His messengers

4: GEOGRAPHICAL PERSPECTIVE

Location of the valley Al-Ahkad between al-Yemen and Oman in Southern Arabia.
Rich land with profuse vegetation, fruits and flowers
The direction of Southern Arabia from the United States.

5: CIVIC PERSPECTIVES

Duties of man towards Allah.
Obedience to the Prophets of Allah

6: LINGUISTIC PERSPECTIVE

Listening; Following directions, Remembering sequences
Oral Language
Reading
Writing

7: ARTISTIC PERSPECTIVE

Finger Plays
Songs and Rhymes
Painting, Coloring, Cutting and Pasting

BIBLIOGRAPHY FOR TEACHERS

1) *Qasas ul Ambiya* in Arabic or Urdu translation
2) Holy Quran (Yusuf Ali's translation)

TIME REQUIREMENTS

Time Needed : 3 - 4 class hours (30 min. each)

Sunday School : 3 lessons (30 min. each)
+ 1 lesson for review and evaluation

Full Time School : 3 lessons (45 min. each)

IQRA' KINDERGARTEN CURRICULUM

ISLAMIC HISTORY

UNIT 3: Prophet Hud (A)

Lesson 1: The People of Aad

FOCAL POINT	PERFORMANCE OBJECTIVES	SUGGESTED ACTIVITIES	RESOURCE MATERIAL
A> History of the children of Adam (A) until Prophet Hud (A)	**The children will:** -recall the history of Islam from the time of Adam (A) to Prophet Hud (A)	**The teacher will:** **a.** Introduce the story by helping the children to recall Iblees's promise to misguide the children of Adam (A). **b.** Show a picture of Nuh's ark to refresh the children's memories of how in the past Allah (SWT) has punished those who disobeyed Him.	Pictures of Nuh's (A) ark
B> Prophet Hud (A) and the people of Aad	-learn that the people of Aad were the descendants of Prophet Nuh (A)	**a.** Tell or read the story of Prophet Hud (A) and the people of Aad who lived many, many years after Prophet Nuh (A). (See A below)	The Storybook of Hud (A)
C> The Timeline of history	-be able to compare and contrast the noble people of Nuh (A), who were on the ark	**a.** Play the sorting by attributes game. (See B below) **b.** Visual discrimination of the different gods that he people of Aad believed in. (See C below)	Game
D> Comparison between the noble ancestors of Aad and the people of Aad at Hud's (A) time.	-be reminded of the flood to show how with time the believers' children lost their ways and faith and began to worship idols.	**a.** Discuss the location where the people of Aad used to live in Southern Arabia between Yemen and Jordan in the valley of Al-Ahkaf.	Map of Arabia
E> SKILLS Visual Discrimination Sequencing Sorting	VOCABULARY Aad Yemen Southern Jordan Al-Ahkaf		

THE STORY OF HUD (A)

The people who sailed with Prophet Nuh (A) were noble Muslims. Some of them settled down in Arabia and lived a pious life. However, as time went by, they changed. They forgot the guidance of Nuh (A) and drifted away from Allah (SWT). They began to worship idols. They used to drink, gamble and cheat each other.

One group of descendants from Nuh (A) were called Aad. They worshipped four different gods. They believed that each of the idols provided them with a different thing. They thought that the first idol brought them rain, the second kept them safe from danger, the third provided them with food, and the fourth one gave them all good health.

So, they believed that all the powers that really belong to Allah (SWT) alone, were divided among these four gods. Instead of worshipping Allah (SWT) *alone*, they were worshipping four different gods *together*! This kind of belief is called *Kufr*. Kufr means covering up or hiding the truth.

The people of Aad were tall, handsome and strong people. They were excellent architects and greatly skilled engineers. They liked building castles and other large structures. They planted beautiful gardens and orchards. But inspite of all these gifts from Allah (SWT), they denied His existence. They believed that their four gods had given them everything. Even though they were great builders, they had no morals. They would cheat, lie, and mistreat each other. They were wicked and disobedient and refused to listen to anyone.

Allah raised a prophet from among them, named Hud (A). Prophet Hud (A) tried to teach the people of Aad that there is only one God, Allah (SWT). He told them again and again to stop worshipping their idols. He begged them to abandon the Kufr and the shirk in their lives. He even warned them about Allah's (SWT) punishment to those who disobey Him, and especially those who associate partners with Allah (SWT). He told them,

"Oh my people! I am not asking for any reward from you. I am simply sent by the Lord of the worlds to warn you and call you back to the path of truth and goodness. If you ask forgiveness from Allah (SWT), and change your ways, He will make you stronger than you are now, give you rain, and accept you, but please, do not continue your evil ways."

The people of Aad were not ready to listen to Prophet Hud (A). They told him, "You're stupid! You're just telling stories of the ancient times. We know that we are not going to be punished and destroyed like the people of Nuh." However, Prophet Hud (A) knew that Allah's punishment would come to his people. After trying to convince them, he decided to leave the valley of Al-Ahkaf, with the people who were Muslims and listened to him.

As soon as Hud (A) left the village, a large cloud appeared in the sky. The people of Aad were happy to see it because it was going to bring rain to their desert land. Little did they know that Allah was sending a terrible windstorm through the cloud - not the rain they were expecting.

The clouds grew larger and larger, as the wind howled louder and louder. The storm raged for seven days and eight nights. The air was full of dust and sand. It became so bad that the people started running to their houses to hide. However, the strong castles and big houses could not save them from the punishment of Allah. The dust filled their houses and their rooms. They could not leave their houses, and as the dust got into their lungs, they died of suffocation.

There was nothing left except the big empty houses of Aad. Even these large, strong houses could not save the people from the punishment of Allah. Their idols could not save them in the least against Allah. The worthless idols that they had worshipped were now completely destroyed and blown away by the storm.

The only people from Aad who were saved from the storm were those who left with Prophet Hud (A). The children of these believers grew up to become good Muslims, who believed in Allah alone and lived pious, righteous lives.

IQRA' KINDERGARTEN CURRICULUM
ISLAMIC HISTORY
Unit 3: Prophet Hud (A)
Lesson 1: The People of Aad
Worksheet C: Visual Discrimination: The Idols of Aad

VISUAL DISCRIMINATION: THE IDOLS OF AAD

The people of Aad were not Muslims. They forgot the teachings of Prophet Nuh (A). They forgot that there is only one God, Allah. Instead they believed in four gods. They believed that:

1) The first god sent them __________.

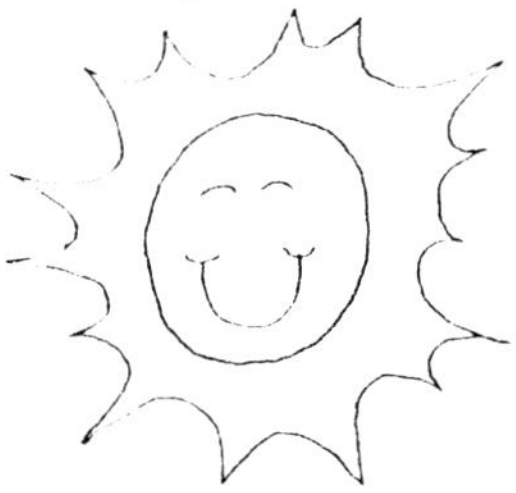

SUNSHINE

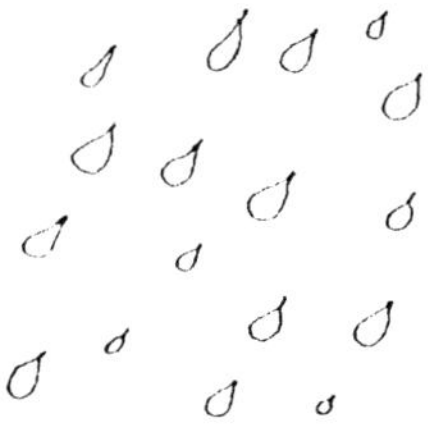

RAIN

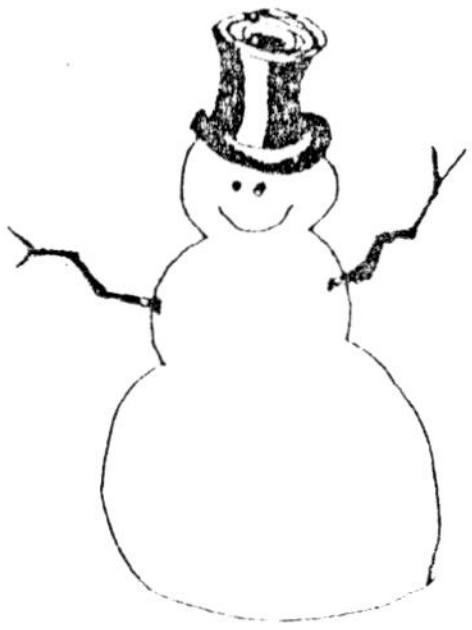

SNOW

2) The second god __________.

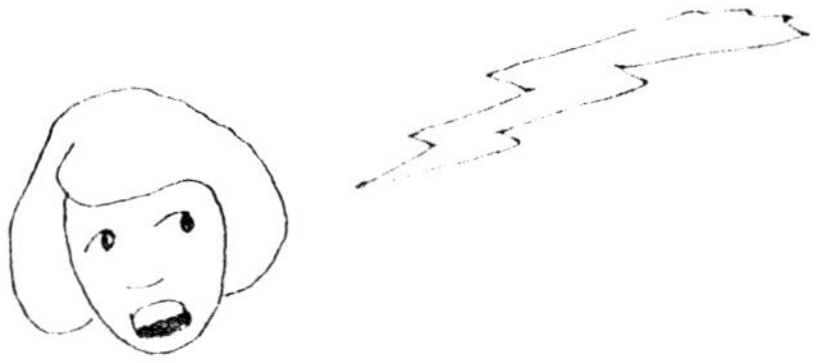

TRIED TO HURT THEM

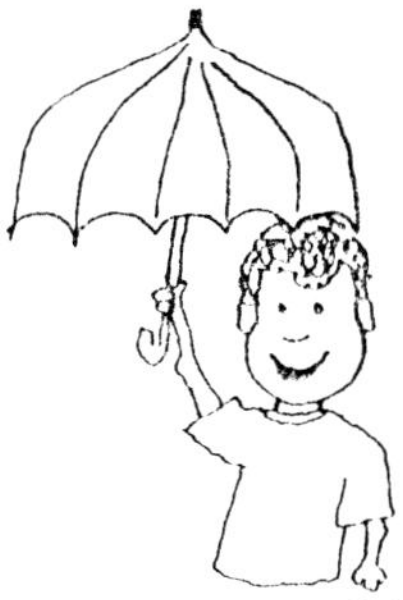

KEPT THEM SAFE

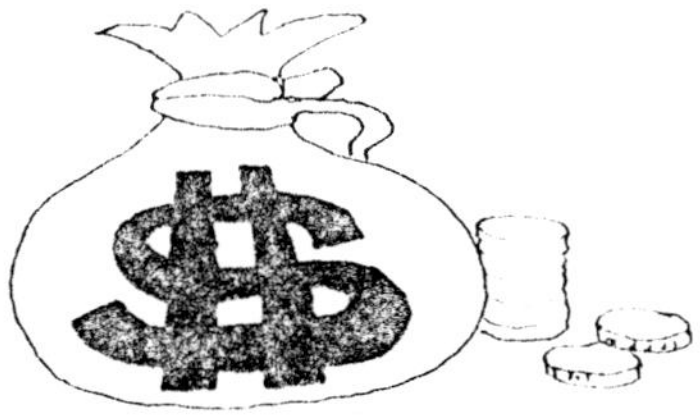

GAVE THEM WEALTH

3) The third god gave them __________.

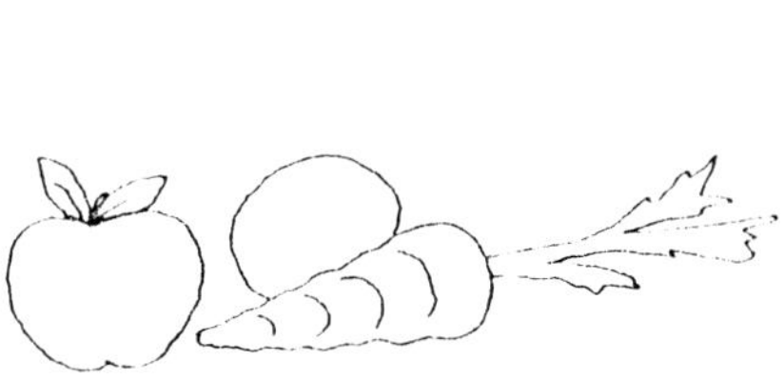

FOOD

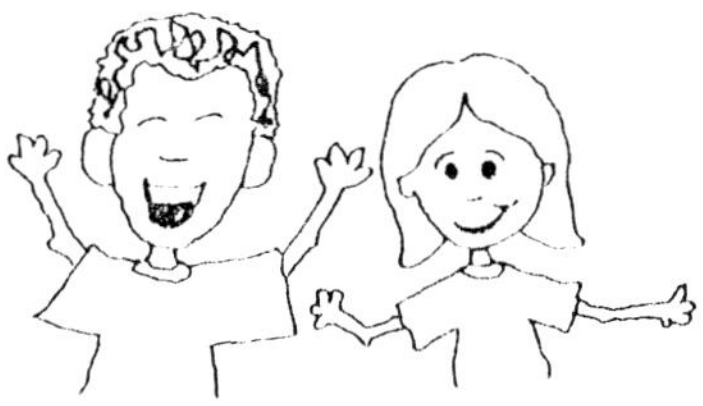

CHILDREN

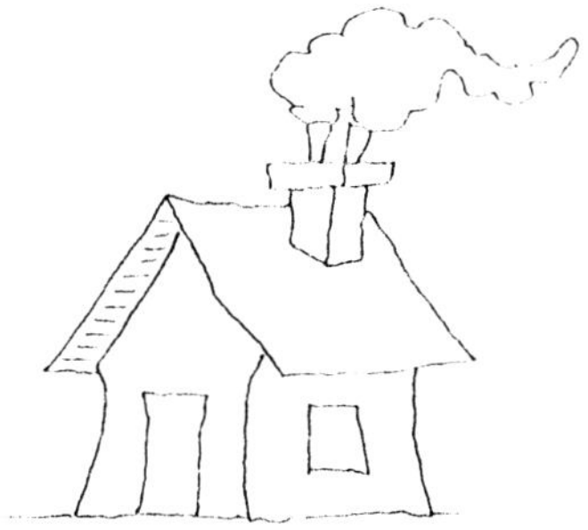

SHELTER

4) The fourth god gave them __________ when they were sick.

CANDY

GOOD HEALTH

MEDICINE

However, all of these four gods were false. They were created by the people of Aad. They did not do anything at all. These gods did not bring the rain which watered the crops. It was not these gods that kept the people safe from danger. It was not these gods that brought the people of Aad food. These fake gods did not cure any of the people who were sick. They did not give them wealth. We, as Muslims, know that these were all blessings from ____________________.

IQRA' KINDERGARTEN CURRICULUM
ISLAMIC HISTORY
UNIT 3: Prophet Hud (A)
Lesson 2: Hud (A), A Prophet of Allah (SWT)

FOCAL POINT	PERFORMANCE OBJECTIVES	SUGGESTED ACTIVITIES	RESOURCE MATERIAL
A> Hud's (A) teachings	**The children will:** -know that Hud (A) was the next prophet after Nuh (A) -use their anticipation and prediction abilities	**The teacher will:** **a.** Talk to the children about the arrogance of the people of Aad. Discuss their beliefs in four different gods. Then tell them about Prophet Hud (A), and his teachings. Talk about the reaction of the people of Aad to his teachings. (See A of previous lesson.) **b.** Ask the children to recall what the people of Prophet Nuh (A) said to him when he warned them about Allah's punishment. Can the children anticipate what will happen to the people of Aad?	
B> Sinners are punished by Allah	-be able to draw conclusions about the punishment of the people of Aad by Allah (SWT)	**a.** Ask the children to guess what kind of punishment Allah would give to the people of Aad (eg. rain, earthquake, etc.) Make a chart of the responses on a large writing pad. (language experience) **b.** After initial discussion, tell the children the rest of the story.	Markers, Writing pad
C> Prophets are always guided by Allah	-be able to anticipate the teachings of Prophet Hud (A) -determine the cause + effect relationship between kufr and shirk, and eventual punishment by Allah (SWT)	**a.** Ask comprehension questions: -Why did the people of Aad not believe Hud (A)? -What do you think could have happened to them as a result of their disobedience? -How many gods did the people of Aad believe in? -Why do you think this is a wrong belief?	

IQRA' KINDERGARTEN CURRICULUM

ISLAMIC HISTORY

UNIT 3: Prophet Hud (A)

Lesson 2: Hud (A), A Prophet of Allah (SWT)
continued . . .

FOCAL POINT	PERFORMANCE OBJECTIVES	SUGGESTED ACTIVITIES	RESOURCE MATERIAL
D> SKILLS	VOCABULARY Punishment Morals Sin Arcitects Castles	**a.** Tell the children to use the vocabulary words in sentences.	

ISLAMIC HISTORY

UNIT 3: Prophet Hud (A)

Lesson 3: The Cloud of Destruction

FOCAL POINT	PERFORMANCE OBJECTIVES	SUGGESTED ACTIVITIES	RESOURCE MATERIAL
A> Allah's (SWT) punishment to the people of Aad.	**The children will:** -know that people who do not obey Allah's prophets are punished -learn, from the story, the virtues of following the right path	**The teacher will:** **a.** Emphasize the calamity which befell the people of Aad, because of their refusal to believe in Allah. **b.** Use the Quran for reference. (Al-Qamar 54 : 18-21) You can have the children memorize these Ayahs with their meanings as homework, and then quiz them on them.	Story of Prophet Hud (A) The Holy Qur'an
B> Causal Relationship between the cloud and the rain	-learn that normally clouds bring rain -rain is always welcomed in a desert because water is so scarce	**a.** Show pictures, slides and films of clouds and rain. Speak of how rain is formed. **b.** Show pictures of the desert and relate the necessity of water for such an arid environment. Ask the children to compare the climate of their home towns with the climate of the desert. Help the children to make a comparative chart of the two.	Pictures and Slides Pictures Posterboard, Markers, Pencils and Paste

FOCAL POINT	PERFORMANCE OBJECTIVES	SUGGESTED ACTIVITIES	RESOURCE MATERIAL
C> Allah (SWT) has control over everything	-learn that the cloud that Allah (SWT) sent to the people of Aad did not bring rain, but a windstorm that that destroyed all of them.	**a.** Discuss with the children how Allah (SWT) can change the phenomenon of nature if He so wills. **b.** Have the children draw conclusions: -Clouds bring _________ (rain) -Sunrise brings _________ (light) -Sunset brings _________ (darkness/light) **c.** Discuss how the people of Aad might not have easily believed that Allah (SWT) would change the cloud into a windstorm, because they did not expect it. We expect everything to go on with a cause/effect relationship, as usual, but Allah (SWT) can do anything. **d.** Ask the children to retell the entire story. **e.** Send the parents of the children progress reports. (See A below)	

PROGRESS REPORT

Dear Parents,

Assalam - u ' Alaikum

GOOD VERY GOOD EXCELLENT

That is how I describe the work your child, ____________________, has done on this unit, which deal with Prophet HUd (A) and the people of Aad. Some of the objectives of this unit have been:

1) To develop a respect for the mission of the prophets of Allah (SWT).

2) To develop an Islamic historical perspective.

3) To help your child develop the ability to discriminate between Iman and Shirk.

4) To help your child develop an understanding of the concepts of different countries beyond the boundaries of their own countries.

5) To help your child develop the ability to compare and contrast.

6) To enhance your child's oral communication skills and widen his/her vocabulary.

Thank You very much for taking the time to read this letter. May the peace and blessings of Allah (SWT) be upon you.

Signed,

____
Kindergarten Teacher

Unit Four: Prophet Salih (A)

lessons 1-3

UNIT FOUR

LEARNING EXPERIENCES AND ACTIVITIES

1: MORAL PERSPECTIVE

Belief in the prophets of Allah (SWT)
Knowledge of the fact that Allah (SWT) has sent His prophets to many people in many lands
Messages of the prophets of Allah (SWT) are for the benefit of mankind
We should always obey the command of Allah (SWT)
Following the teachings of the prophets of Allah (SWT)
These stories of the prophets are mentioned in the Quran as warnings to us
All the guidance of the prophets still exists today

2: HISTORICAL PERSPECTIVE

Timeline from Prophet Adam (A) to Prophet Salih (A)
Thamud : The people of Salih (A)
Some verses of the Quran which describe the story (Surah Al-Shams: 91)

3: GEOGRAPHICAL PERSPECTIVE

Location of the homeland of the people of Thamud (between Makkah and Madinah)
Scarcity of water in the desert climate
The means of travel in the desert during the time of Salih (A)

4: LINGUISTIC PERSPECTIVE

Language experience stories
Oral language, Listening, Vocabulary
Writing and Reading

5: ARTISTIC PERSPECTIVE

Singing
Acting
Cutting and Pasting
Painting

CONCLUSION

EVALUATION

TIME REQUIREMENTS

Time Needed: 4 Class hours (30-35 min. each)

Sunday School: 3 Class hours (30-45 min. each)

Full Time School: 4 Class hours (30-45 min. each)

IQRA' KINDERGARTEN CURRICULUM

ISLAMIC HISTORY

UNIT 4: Prophet Salih (A)

Lesson 1: Thamud; The People of Salih (A)

FOCAL POINT	PERFORMANCE OBJECTIVES	SUGGESTED ACTIVITIES	RESOURCE MATERIAL
A> Thamud, the people of Arabia	**The children will:** -learn that the people of Thamud lived near Madinah and came from a small band that escaped the destruction of Aad	**The teacher will:** **a.** Introduce the story. (See A below). Start the story by telling the children, "About 200 years after the destruction of Aad, Allah (SWT) sent another prophet to the people in Arabia." **b.** Ask the children if they have ever been to Madinah in Saudi Arabia. Why is Madinah such a famous city? Show the children a picture of Madinah. **c.** Using a map of Saudi Arabia, locate Madinah-Al-Salih with the children. Talk about the direction, using north to south and west to east bearings.	Pictures Map of Saudi Arabia Compass
B> The people of Thamud were disbelievers	-learn that the people of Thamud were not good people	**a.** Discuss with the children the implications of the beliefs of the people of Thamud and then compare and contrast them with the beliefs of Muslims. (Critical Thinking and Comparison Evaluation) **b.** Help the children to relate the disobedience (to Allah's law) of the people of Thamud with the people of Aad and the people of Nuh (A).	

IQRA' KINDERGARTEN CURRICULUM
ISLAMIC HISTORY
Unit 4: Prophet Salih (A)
Lesson 1: Thamud, the people of Prophet Salih (A)
Worksheet A: The Story of Prophet Salih (A)

PROPHET SALIH (A) AND THE PEOPLE OF THAMUD

The people of Thamud were the descendants of those people of Aad, who survived Allah's (SWT) punishment and followed the teachings of Prophet Hud (A). They used to live in the valley of Qura, which is located in Arabia. It is also called Fajjul-Naqa.

Allah (SWT) gave many comforts to the people of Thamud. They were blessed with beautiful gardens with lovely flowers and rich orchards filled with all kinds of fruits. There were rivers of clear, clean water flowing through the valley and graceful tall mountains surrounding the valley.

The people of Thamud were beautiful and strong people. Allah (SWT) had given them a special gift through their ability of building and designing houses in the mountains. They were exceptional architects and engineers.

They used to make beautiful houses and buildings by cutting the mountains. They could cut and shape mountain stone like it was wax. The people of Thamud were famous for their stone carvings and architecture. People from far way lands used to visit their beautiful city.

As time passed the people of Thamud forgot the teachings of both Prophet Hud (A) and Prophet Nuh (A). They became arrogant and proud. They began to believe that they were the most powerful people on earth and thought they could do anything they wanted to. They became insolent people.

They forgot that everything is created by Allah (SWT) and He is the most powerful. They did not believe that if Allah (SWT) wanted He could destroy everything, including their city, with all its marvelous buildings and lovely gardens.

The people of Thamud began to think that they were going to live forever and that they were safe in their houses. They became ignorant and began worshipping idols instead of Allah (SWT) alone. They began to make different idols, gave them names, and started bowing in front of them, asking them for everything, and then worship them as their gods.

At this time Allah (SWT) decided to send a prophet to teach these people just like He had sent to the people of Prophet Nuh(A) and Prophet Hud(A).

Allah (SWT) sent Prophet Salih (A) to the people of Thamud. Prophet Salih was a very noble, pious and very intelligent man. Every one knew him for his good nature and intelligence. He used to respect his elders and love the young. He was helpful to everyone. His father was very proud of him and used to think that his son Salih would grow up to be a rich man and everyone would respect him and listen to his commands. But Allah (SWT) had a different plans for Prophet Salih.

Allah (SWT) wanted Prophet Salih (A) to bring his people out of the darkness of ignorance. He asked Prophet Salih (A) to teach the people of Thamud to:

"*Worship only Allah.*"

And to tell them that:

"There is no God but Allah (SWT). He is the only one we should worship. We should bow our heads to Him alone. We should ask only from Him, and we should trust Him."

Prophet Salih (A) told his people that he was the messenger of Allah (SWT) and Allah had sent him to teach them about the right path. Prophet Salih (A) told his people that he was their brother and their friend and whatever he was telling them was for their own good. He requested that they listen to what he was saying and give up their bad habits of cheating, lying, drinking and idol worship.

There were a small number of people who believed in Prophet Salih's (A) teachings and became his followers. But most of them did not want to pay any attention to what he was saying. They refused to change their evil ways. One day people of Thamud told Prophet Salih (A) that they thought he was a magician and they were not going to listen to him unless he brought some special sign which could show that he is telling the truth.

Prophet Salih (A) asked them, "What sign do you want to see?"

They replied, "If you are a true Prophet, O Salih, then try to make a she-camel appear from underneath this mountain. Then make her deliver a baby camel as soon as she comes out of the mountain."

They thought that a she-camel could never come out from the mountain, because a camel can only be born from its mother. They were sure that Prophet Salih (A) would never be able to fulfill such a condition. They thought he would feel ashamed and stop telling everyone to worship only Allah (SWT).

But, the people of Thamud were not aware of Allah's (SWT) power. They did not know that when Allah (SWT) wants to do something He does it right away in a moment. Nothing is impossible for Allah (SWT), as He has power over everything and everyone. But Prophet Salih (A) knew this, so he prayed to Allah and said, "O Allah, show them whatever they want to see."

Allah (SWT) listened to Prophet Salih's (A) prayer and all of a sudden the mountain opened and a she-camel came out. She delivered a baby as soon as she came out of the mountain. The people were surprised and shocked, it took them a while to believe what they saw.

However, most of the people still did not believe Prophet Salih A). Prophet Salih A) told the people that the she-camel was a sign from Allah (SWT) and they had to protect her and share the water and the grass with her. They agreed to let her drink the water from the river one day and their animals the other day.

There were some cruel people who did not like the she-camel and, inspite of Prophet Salih's warning, they decided to kill her. One day they actually killed the she-camel.

When Prophet Salih (A) came to know about the plight of the she-camel he became very sad and angry. He warned his people about Allah's (SWT) punishment. He told them, "You are unfortunate people because you could not be patient. You disobeyed Allah (SWT). Now you wait for Allah's (SWT) punishment. After three days, the punishment will come and destroy all of you."

The people of Thamud were very scared, because they did not want to die.. From the morning the signs of Allah's punishment began to appear. The faces of the people of Thamud began to turn yellow with the fear, the next day they all became so scared that their faces turned red and then dark due to the fear of death. They knew that they were going to receive Allah's punishment. The also knew in their hearts that Prophet Salih (A) was right in his techings but they did not want to accept the fact.

After three days and nights the time of the night arrived when a strong earthquake with extremely loud sound hit their city and killed everyone living there. Prophet Salih (A) and his followers were saved and protected by Allah (SWT) . Prophet Salih left his people saying;

> O my people! I did indeed convey to you the message
> for which I was sent by my Lord: I gave you good counsel,
> but ye love not good counsellors. (Surah 7:Ayah 79)

IQRA' KINDERGARTEN CURRICULUM
ISLAMIC HISTORY
UNIT 4: Prophet Salih (A)
Lesson 2: Prophet Salih (A) Invites his people to *Tawhid*

FOCAL POINT	PERFORMANCE OBJECTIVES	SUGGESTED ACTIVITIES	RESOURCE MATERIAL
A> Prophet Salih (A), a messenger to the people of Thamud	**The children will:** -know the name and mission of Prophet Salih (A) -believe that Salih (A) was a true prophet of Allah (SWT)	**The teacher will:** **a.** Finish reading or telling the story of Thamud.	Story of Prophet Salih (A)
B> Teachings of Prophet Salih (A)	-believe in the teachings of Salih (A)	**a.** Tell the children of Prophet Salih's (A) teachings so that the children can recall and relate the teachings themselves. The teacher should make a chart to display later on in the class.	
C> Disobedience	-learn that the people of Thamud did not listen to the command of Allah (SWT) and killed the she-camel	**a.**Make a worksheet about Prophet Salih (A) and Prophet Hud (A).	

IQRA' KINDERGARTEN CURRICULUM
ISLAMIC HISTORY
UNIT 4: Prophet Salih (A)
Lesson 3: The Punishment from Allah (SWT)

FOCAL POINT	PERFORMANCE OBJECTIVES	SUGGESTED ACTIVITIES	RESOURCE MATERIAL
A> The disobedience of the people of Thamud to Allah (SWT)	**The children will:** -know that the people of Thamud rejected the teachings of Prophet Salih (A) and killed the she-camel	**The teacher will:** **a.** Tell the children the story of Prophet Salih (A) and the people's rejection of his teachings. **b.** Discuss how the people of Thamud wanted to kill Prophet Salih (A).	
B> Disobedience is punished	-know that Allah destroyed the disobedient people of Thamud with a volcanic eruption, but the people of Kin'an escaped	**a.** Discuss natural phenomenons, focusing on volcanoes. **b.** Show pictures and films of volcanoes to help the children understand the powers of nature and Allah.	Pictures, Films
C> Forces of nature are controlled by Allah (SWT)	-be able to compare the strong winds which destroyed the people of Aad to the volcanic eruptions which destroyed the people of Thamud	**a.** Help the children to recall the ways in which Allah punished the people of Nuh (A) and the people of Aad for their disobedience. **b.** Make a listening discrimination exercise sheet based on the stories of the three prophets studied thus far, and their people. (See A below) **c.** The children can draw pictures of volcanoes.	Paper, Crayons, Markers
D> The stories of the prophets are told in the Quran	-know that the these stories are true because they are in the Quran	**a.** Read Surah Al-Shams to the children in Arabic. Discuss the meaning of the surah in English and how it relates to Prophet Salih (A) and the people of Thamud. **a.** Help the children memorize this Surah.	Qur'an

IQRA' KINDERGARTEN CURRICULUM

ISLAMIC HISTORY

UNIT 4: Prophet Salih (A)

Lesson 3: The Punishment from Allah (SWT)

continued . . .

FOCAL POINT	PERFORMANCE OBJECTIVES	SUGGESTED ACTIVITIES	RESOURCE MATERIAL
E> SKILLS	VOCABULARY Thamud Refused Volcano Eruption Lava	**a.** Provide practice in vocabulary development **b.** Use the vocabulary in future lessons and stories and integrate the vocabulary words in the lectures and discussions of other classes (ie. Science, Social Studies, etc.) **c.** Send a progress report home to the parents of the children. (See B below)	

IQRA' KINDERGARTEN CURRICULUM
ISLAMIC HISTORY
Unit 4: Prophet Salih (A)
Lesson 3: The Punishment from Allah (SWT)
Worksheet A: Progress Report

PROGRESS REPORT

Dear Parents,

Assalam-u 'Alaikum

GOOD VERY GOOD EXCELLENT

That is how I describe the work your child, ____________________________, has done on this unit, which dealt with Prophet Salih (A) and the people of Thamud. Some of the objectives of the unit have been:

1) To help the children develop an understanding of the roles the prophets of Allah (SWT).

2) To familiarize the children with the mission and teachings of Prophet Salih (A).

3) To develop an Islamic historical perspective.

4) To help the children develop an understanding of the cause and effect relationship between disobedience to Allah (SWT) and His punishment.

Thank you for taking the time to read this letter. May the peace and blessings of Allah (SWT) be upon you and your family.

Signed,

____
Kindergarten Teacher

Unit Five: Prophet Ibrahim (A)

lessons 1-6

UNIT FIVE

LEARNING EXPERIENCES AND ACTIVITIES

1: MORAL PERSPECTIVE

Allah (SWT) is the only Creator
He is the only Protector
Allah (SWT) helps those who ask His protection
Concept of shirk and idol worship
Punishment for shirk
Belief in the ultimate victory of the truth
Obedience to Allah (SWT) is the basic requirement of faith
Love of a mother towards her son
Obedience to parents

2: SOCIAL PERSPECTIVES

Sharing and working with each other
Need for cooperation
Basic necessities of life (food, water, shelter, etc.)
Love for family and friends
People from different tribes, families and countries are all created by Allah, and are thus one equal nation

3: HISTORICAL PERSPECTIVE

The people of Iraq and Palestine: the idol worshippers
The role of kings in ancient civilization
The history of the city of Makkah
The building of the Kabah
The foundations of Allah (SWT) religion; Islam

4: GEOGRAPHICAL PERSPECTIVE

Locations of Egypt, Iraq, and Palestine, and Saudi Arabia and their specific landmarks.
The desert and its specific features (heat, lack of water, desert plants, etc.)
The development of the city of Makkah
The north and south trade route through Saudi Arabia

5: LINGUISTIC AND COGNITIVE PERSPECTIVE

Vocabulary
Comprehension
Language development
Listening skills
Sequencing
Cause and effect relationships
Drawing conclusions
Comparing and contrasting
Raising questions and searching for the answers

6: ARTISTIC PERSPECTIVE

Singing
Finger Puppets
Music and Movement
Painting and Coloring
Cutting and Pasting

CONCLUSION

EVALUATION

TIME REQUIREMENTS

Time Needed : 6 - 7 class hours (30 min. each)

Sunday School : 6 Lessons (30 min. each)

Full Time School : 5 - 6 Lessons (45 min. each)

IQRA' KINDERGARTEN CURRICULUM
ISLAMIC HISTORY
UNIT 5: PROPHET IBRAHIM (A)
Lesson 1: The Idol Worshippers

FOCAL POINT	PERFORMANCE OBJECTIVES	SUGGESTED ACTIVITIES	RESOURCE MATERIAL
A> The ignorant idol worshippers	**The children will:** -know that Allah (SWT) is not pleased with those people who worship idols	**The teacher will:** **a.** Read or tell the children about the king Namrood and the idol worshippers of Iraq at the time of Ibrahim's (A) birth. (See A below)	Story of Prophet Ibrahim (A)
B> Mushrik and Kafir	-Learn that idol worshippers are called Kafirun	**a.** Pinpoint the location of Iraq on the world map and discuss the earlier mentioned country of Prophet Nuh (A). **b.** Talk about the direction of Iraq from the United States (or your country). **c.** Give the name of the actual place Ibrahim (A) lived.	World Map
C> Ibrahim's (A) father, Azar	-learn the name of his father -learn that he used to make idols	**a.** Talk of Ibrahim (A) as a young boy. Include discussions of his father, the idol carver, and the people of Kannan, who worshipped idols. **b.** Tell the story of how Ibrahim (A) broke all the idols in the Kabah, and put the sword in the hands of the biggest one.	Quran 26: 69 - 102 21: 51 - 72 29: 16 - 19 37: 83 - 99 43: 26 - 28 60: 3 - 4
D> Obedience to parents is conditional on their *Iman*	-learn to reject any beliefs that are UnIslamic	**a.** Have an open discussion with the children on obedience to parents, showing how Ibrahim's (A) disobedience to his father, by refusing to worship idols was justified.	Quran 60: 3 - 4
continued next page			

FOCAL POINT	PERFORMANCE OBJECTIVES	SUGGESTED ACTIVITIES	RESOURCE MATERIAL
E> When Allah (SWT) wants to save someone, nobody can harm that individual or group	-learn that Prophet Ibrahim (A) was a true believer in Allah (SWT)	**a.** Discuss the incidence of the king's order.	

IQRA' KINDERGARTEN CURRICULUM
ISLAMIC HISTORY
Unit 5: Prophet Ibrahim (A)
Lesson 1: The Idol Worshippers
Worksheet A: King Namrood and the Idol Worshippers

In a country called Mesopotamia, (now called Iraq) there lived an idol carver named Azar. Azar used to carve idols from wood and stone to sell them to poeple as gods. People of Mesopotamia were idol worshippers, which means that they used to pray to idols made of wood or stone and call them gods. They believed that those idols had power over every thing.

Azar had a son, named Ibrahim who was very different than the rest of the people in the country. He could not understand how idols, which are made by the people themselves could be gods. He was a very intelligent he used to ask questions about the beliefs and practices of his people. One day, he asked his father ," O, my father why do you worship that which neither sees, hears nor does any thing for you?" "O my father! serve not Satan , for Satan is a rebel against Allah, most Gracious" (Surah 19:42 & 44)

Azar got very angry at his son's questions and told Ibrahim;

> " Do you hate my gods, O Ibrahim? If you do not forbear, I will indeed stone you to death. Now, get away from me for a good long while."
>
> (19:46)

Ibrahim (A) became very distressed with his father's thinking. He would think all the time who has created the world? Who is the real God? Besides worshipping idols, people of Iraq during the times of Prophet Ibrahim used to worship the stars, the moon and the sun also. Allah (SWT) wanted Prophet Ibrahim to stay away from Shirk and believe only in one God, Allah, so He made him look at the stars, the moon and the sun and realize that they could not be gods. Once "when the darkness of the night spread all over, Ibrahim saw the shining stars and thought that was his god." but when the stars died he said, " no, I do not like those who disappear, this can not be the god." Then he saw the shining moon and said, " this is my Lord." but when the moon set, he said "no, this is not my god. If my Allah would not have shown me the straight path, I would have been one of the lost people." In the morning he saw the bright sun rise and said "This is my Lord, this is the biggest one of all", but it was not long when even the sun sat. Ibrahim (A) realized that none of these earthly things are the Creator of the world. He said to his people;

> O my people, I am tired of all those things which you associate with God. I have associated myself with Allah, Who (is not created by anyone) has created the sky and the earth. And I am not one of those who make partners with Allah (SWT).

Ibrahim (A) found the answer that Allah (SWT) is the great God. He has created the star, the moon, the sun, the earth and every thing else. He went to the market place and called to the people and asked them' " To whom do you pray?' " They said that they prayed to the idols which were worshipped by their fathers and grandfathers before them. Ibrahim (A) told them, " You, your fathers and your grandfathers are wrong. These idols are not gods."

Ibrahim (A) kept on telling his people that they were wrong to worship the idols, the stars, the moon and the sun. He told them to worship only one God, Allah. People did not listen to him and made fun of him. One day when people had gone to a fair, Ibrahim (A) stayed behind. He thought of plan to make his people understand that the idols were helpless stones or wood figures who had no power. He picked up a hammer and went to the place where all the idols were kept for worship and broke all of them except the largest one. He hanged the hammer in the neck of that one and left.

When the people returned from the fair and found all their idols broken except for one, they became very angry. They knew that Ibrahim (A) was responsible for breaking their idols, they called him and asked him, "Are you the one, who has done this to our gods, O Ibrahim?" Ibrahim (A) replied, " No, this was done by -- This is their biggest one ! Ask them, if they can speak intelligently!" (21:63)

The people were ashamed, they kept their eyes down and replied, "Ibrahim, you know that these idols do not speak.". Prophet Ibrahim(A) then told them, "Do you then worship, besides Allah, things that can neither be of any good to you nor do you any harm? Shame on you, and upon the things that you worship besides Allah! Have you no sense?"(21:66-67).

Prophet Ibrahim (A) asked them to stop worshipping the idols, the stars, the moon and sun. The king of Mesopotamia was called Nimrod. He used to believe that he was a god and made his people worship him and obey him all the time. When Nimrod found out about Prophet Ibrahim (A) and his teachings, he became very worried and angry . He thought that if the people began to follow Prophet Ibrahim (A), they would not believe in Nimrod as god and he will lose his power and his kingdom. The king and other powerful people in the country began plans to stop Prophet Ibrahim from telling the truth about Allah, the only Creator.

Then one day they decided to build a huge fire in one place and burn prophet Ibrahim (A) in the fire. The people built a huge fire which continued to burn for a few days until the king became sure that there would be no way for Prophet Ibrahim to escape the fire. Then the people captured Prophet Ibrahim (A) and threw him in the midst of the burning flames. But at that very moment, Allah (SWT) who has given fire the power to burn, ordered it to save Ibrahim (A) from its burning effects and cool down for him. Allah (SWT) says in the Qur'an ;

"O fire!be thou cool and (a means of) safety for Ibrahim"

(Surah 21:Ayah 69)

When people saw Prophet Ibrahim (A) walking out of the burning fire without a single scratch, they were shocked. However, they were stubborn and did not want to believe in Allah (SWT) as the only Creator. They kept on hurting Prophet Ibrahim (A). Finally, he decided to migrate to some other country where people would follow his teachings and believe in only one Allah. Prophet Ibrahim, his wife Sarah and his nephew, Lut (A) and his wife packed their baggage and started to go to the land of Palestine with Allah's guidance. The family stayed in Palestine for a while and then travelled to many other places till they reached Egypt. They stayed in Egypt for a little while, the King of Egypt became so impressed with the nobility of Prophet Ibrahim (A) and the piety of his wife, Sarah that he sent his daughter Hajjar to live with them and serve them. The family travelled back to Palestine and settled there. Prophet Ibrahim married Hajjar on the recommendation of Sarah as the couple wanted to have children and Sarah could not bear any child.

Allah (SWT) gave good news of a son to Prophet Ibrahim (A) and Hajjar. One day Hazrat Hajjar dreamed that an angel was telling her that she would have a baby boy who will be the leader of the people and they should call him Ismaeel. When the baby boy was born Prophet Ibrahim called him Ismaeel. They loved their son very much. They thanked Allah (SWT) for blessing them with Ismaeel. "

THE BIRTH OF ISMAEEL (A) AND JOURNEY TO MAKKAH

Prophet Ibrahim (A) and Hazrat Hajjar were very happy in their home in Palestine with their young son. Allah (SWT) had great plans for Hazrat Hajjar and her son, Ismaeel, who was to become a prophet of Allah. Allah asked Prophet Ibrahim to take his son Ismaeel and wife Hajjar to the valley of Makkah in Arabia. Prophet Ibrahim (A) asked Hazrat Hajjar to get ready to travel with him and the baby.

They travelled a long way to the land of Arabia, Hajjar kept on asking her husband ,"how much farther we have to go?'It was a long ride on the back of a camel till they reached to the valley of Makkah. Prophet Ibrahim (A) stopped the camel asked him to sit down and helped his wife to dismount the camel. He got the baby down. They sat down on the sandy desert ground and rested a little. As Hajjar looked around she saw hot sandy desert with no shady trees , water or even human in sight. It was very lonely . Prophet Ibrahim (A) gave Hazrat Hajjar a bag of water and some dates to keep when they feel hungry and thirsty. Then he told her that he has to leave her and the baby alone in that desert and return back to Palestine. She was shocked to hear the news that he was going to leave her alone with their only baby son.

As Prophet Ibrahim (A) started to walk away from them, she followed him asking him' " Where are you going leaving us alone in this barren place where there is no human being and nothing to eat or drink?" but Prophet Ibrahim kept on walking away without answering her quarries. He was very sad to leave his family alone but he had to follow

Allah's commands. He had full trust that Allah (SWT) would take care of his family. After a while Hazrat Hajjar asked him, " Is this the command of Allah (SWT) to leave us here alone?" Prophet Ibrahim (A) turned around and told her, "Yes, this is Allah's order". When Hazrat Hajjar heard this she said, "if this is the command of Allah (SWT) then surely He is not going to destroy us" and returned to the place where they sat before. Prophet Ibrahim (A) kept on walking away with a heavy heart till he reached a place from where he could not see his family any more, he stopped on a hill and prayed to Allah (SWT) by saying,

> O, our Lord! I have made some of my offspring to dwell
> in a valley without cultivation, by Thy Sacred House
> In order, O our Lord, that they may establish regular
> Prayer: so fill the hearts of some among men with
> love towards them, and feed them with fruits: so
> that they may give thanks. (Surah 14: Ayah 37)

BUILDING THE HOUSE OF ALLAH

Allah (SWT) told Prophet Ibrahim (A) and his son Ismaeel to build His House in the valley of Makkah. This House of Allah is called Kabah. Prophet Ibrahim (A) and his son Isameel (A) built the Kabah with rocks and stones. When the walls were raised high enough,angel Jibril (A) came to the Prophets and helped them to place the Balckstone (Hajr al Aswad) in its place. The Black Stone is still there in the wall of the Kabah. This stone was sent to earth from Heaven by Allah (SWT).

When the building of the Kabah was ready Allah (SWT) told Prophet Ibrahim and Prophet Ismaeel that it was the place of worship for all Muslims who believe in only one God, Allah and in His messengers. He also told that people from all over the world would come and go around the Kabah in praise of Allah (SWT)

Prophet Ibrahim (A) prayed to Allah (SWT) to bless him and all the Muslims with Iman and show them the right path. He asked Allah (SWT) to have mercy on the people who would come to live in Makkah and visit the Kabah and provide all kinds of fruits and vegetables for them.

llah (SWT) heard Prophet Ibrahim's prayers and even now Muslims from all over the world come to Makkah to do Tawaf of Kabah and praise Allah (SWT) as the only God. The number of Muslims who go to Makkah to perform Hajj or Umra grows every year. Allah (SWT) has asked every Muslim to visit Kabah at least once in his or her lifetime and perform Hajj . Let us pray that Allah (SWT) helps us also to go to Makkah and perform Hajj InshaAllah.

IQRA' KINDERGARTEN CURRICULUM

ISLAMIC HISTORY

UNIT 5: PROPHET IBRAHIM (A)

Lesson 2: The Migration with Sarah and Lut

FOCAL POINT	PERFORMANCE OBJECTIVES	SUGGESTED ACTIVITIES	RESOURCE MATERIAL
A> Migration (Hijrah) in the way of Allah (SWT)	**The children will:** -learn that Prophet Ibrahim (A) left his country and travelled to Palestine -his wife, Sara, and nephew, Lut, accompanied him because they believed in his message	**The teacher will:** **a.** Use a large map of the Middle East to illustrate the path Ibarahim (A) took to migrate to Palestine. **b.** Discuss the concepts of near and distant, using a map. For example: -Palestine is to the (north, south, east, west) of the Tigris River, which is to the (north, south, east, west) of Jordan etc. **c.** Make this a listening exercise for the class, giving directions for the children to follow.	Map of the Middle East Story of the Prophet Ibrahim (A) Worksheets with the map of the Middle East, with arrows pointing to the north, south, east, west.
B> Obedience to Allah (SWT) alone is required of all Muslims	-learn that we <u>must</u> follow Allah's (SWT) command as Muslims -learn to follow Ibrahim's (A) Sunnat of obeying Allah (SWT) all the time	**a.** Discuss the difficulty and hardships of moving to a new place. Talk about the experiences of children who have moved, and their feelings after leaving their home and their friends. **b.** Discuss the means of transportation Ibrahim (A) and his family could have used to move. (Historical Perspective) **c.** Show pictures of people moving, to generate a discussion about leaving a well known place to settle down in another.	
C> <u>SKILLS</u>	<u>VOCABULARY</u> Sunnat Obey Allah		

IQRA' KINDERGARTEN CURRICULUM
ISLAMIC HISTORY
UNIT 5: PROPHET IBRAHIM (A)
Lesson 3: The Birth of Ismail and the Journey to Makkah

FOCAL POINT	PERFORMANCE OBJECTIVES	SUGGESTED ACTIVITIES	RESOURCE MATERIAL
A> The love of Allah (SWT) is supreme for a Muslim	**The children will:** -learn that Prophet Ibrahim (A) trusted Allah (SWT) -learn that Prophet Ibrahim's (A) wives also loved Allah (SWT)	**The teachers will:** **a.** Tell the story of Prophet Ibrahim's (A) marriage to Hazrat Hajar on the insistence of Hazrat Sara, the birth of Ismail, and Allah's command to leave them both in the valley of Makkah.	
B> Allah (SWT) rewards those who trust in Him	-learn that Prophet Ibrahim's (A) wish to have a child was fulfilled by Allah (SWT) twice	**a.** Talk about the happiness of the family at the birth of the new baby. Ask children with younger siblings to relate such experiences. **b.** Write down the experience stories: *I had a baby brother/sister* _____	
C> Obedience to Allah (SWT) is expected of all Muslims	-learn that at the time, Makkah was a very barren place	**a.** Talk about the barren, unfertile and uninhabited desert of *Bakkah*, compared to the fertile, populated land of Palestine. **b.** Talk about the fear of being alone in a deserted place. Let the children relate their feelings on being alone, with the feelings of Hazrat Hajar. **c.** Write a language experience story with the children in a group setting: *If I were alone in a desert* _________.	
continued next page			

<table>
<tr>
<td>D> Obedience and trust in Allah (SWT) is rewarded</td>
<td>-be able to relate to the feelings of Hazrat Hajar's trust in Allah, (SWT) and her willingness to obey Allah (SWT)</td>
<td>a. Discuss the trust Hazrat Hajar had in Allah, and her willingness to obey her husband.

b. Use the topic to generate oral language and discussion among children.

c. Ask inferential and critical comprehension questions. (See examples below)

d. Help the children to memorize Prophet Ibrahim's (A) dua' before leaving his wife and child in the valley of Makkah.

"My Lord! Make safe this territory and preserve me and my sons from serving idols." (Surah XIV:25)</td>
<td></td>
</tr>
<tr>
<td>E> <u>SKILLS</u></td>
<td><u>VOCABULARY</u>
Safe
Preserve
Territory
Barren</td>
<td><u>Comprehension Questions</u>

a. Why did Prophet Ibrahim (A) leave Harat Hajar and the baby in the valley of Makkah?

b. How did Hazrat Hajar feel about being left alone?

c. How did Prophet Ibrahim (A) feel about leaving his family in a lonely place?

d. Why was Ibrahim (A) sure that Allah (SWT) would help his family and take care of them?</td>
<td></td>
</tr>
</table>

Lesson 4: Zamzam; Allah's Reward to Hazrat Hajar

FOCAL POINT	PERFORMANCE OBJECTIVES	SUGGESTED ACTIVITIES	RESOURCE MATERIAL
A> Allah (SWT) is merciful and compassionate	**The children will:** -learn that mothers care more for their children than they do for themselves	**The teacher will:** **a.** Read or tell the story of Hajar and her baby Ismail,when the water ran out after Prophet Ibrahim (A) left them. (See A below) **b.** Emphasize the extreme love of Hazrat Hajar for her baby, Ismael.	
B> Allah (SWT) is the Provider	-learn that Hazrat Hajar was the founder of Makkah	**a.** Provide the children with some experience of hunger and thirst by delaying the snack or lunch time by an hour or so. Talk about the feelings of hunger and thirst and relate them to the feelings of Hajar in the heat of Makkah.	
C> The mother's love for her children is Allah's (SWT) gift	-learn that Hazrat Hajar trusted Allah (SWT)for help and protection.	**a.** Discuss the needs of water for human beings, animals, plants, etc. with the children.	
D> Water is essential for life	-learn that plants need water to grow	**a.** Plan for the following activities in advance: -Place two or more plants on a sunny windowsill. Give water to only one of the plants, and leave the other one dry. After three or four days compare the two plants to prove the necessity of water for life. -During the summer time, put a bird bath outside the window so the children can see the birds play and drink in the water. Also bring in some classroom pets and have the children in charge of giving a constant supply of water and food.	Plants and Water Bird Bath
continued next page			

IQRA' KINDERGARTEN CURRICULUM

ISLAMIC HISTORY

UNIT 5: PROPHET IBRAHIM (A)

Lesson 4: Zamzam; Allah's Reward to Hazrat Hajrah

. . . continued . . .

FOCAL POINT	PERFORMANCE OBJECTIVES	SUGGESTED ACTIVITIES	RESOURCE MATERIAL
E> Lack of water causes drought	-know the cause and effect relationship between water and life	**a.** Show films and pictures of the drought in Ethiopia to illustrate the effects of a severe lack of water. Then, for comparison, show pictures of rainforests and woods filled with animals. **b.** Conclude with the children that Hazrat Hajrah was happy to have Zamzam in the desert. Mention that the thirsty birds also started to come and drink from the stream. **c.** Help the children to make a mural of desert birds. Underneath the drawing or picture of each bird, write its name for vocabulary and reading exercise.	Films and Photographs Pictures and cut outs of birds
F> A mother's love for her baby	-learn that Hajar ran back and forth in search of water for her crying baby. -get the experience of exhaustion from running between Saffa and Marwa	**a.** Take the children to the playground and have them walk back and forth seven times between two points, to feel the exhaustion and tiredness. Afterwards, talk about the experience. During rugtime, write down language experience stories about the experience. Ask the children to illustrate the stories they tell. **b.** Take the children to the sandbox and have them recreate the hills of Saffa and Marwa. Otherwise, guide the children as they make models of the hills out of clay.	
continued next page			

IQRA' KINDERGARTEN CURRICULUM

ISLAMIC HISTORY

UNIT 5: PROPHET IBRAHIM (A)

Lesson 4: Zamzam; Allah's (SWT) Reward to Hazrat Hajrah

. . . continued . . .

G> SKILLS Cause and Effect Drawing Conclusions Compare and Contrast	VOCABULARY Zamzam Desert Drought		

THE STORY OF ZAMZAM

After Prophet Ibrahim (A) left, Hazrat Hajar sat, holding her baby son and praying to Allah (SWT). Soon, her supply of water was gone. She started to worry about how she was going to keep the baby and herself alive without any water. Soon, Ismail became very thirsty, and he began to cry. Hazrat Hajar did not know what to do. She put the baby down on the ground and started looking for water.

There were two hills nearby, called Saffa and Marwa. She climbed onto Saffa to look for water. When she did not find any water there, she ran to Marwa to look for water. However, she didn't find any water there either. She could hear her baby crying with thirst. She ran back to the first hill, Saffa, again, but did not find any water. She could hear Ismail crying even louder, so she became desperate and worried. She ran back to the second hill, Marwa, but could still find no water. She continued to run back and forth, but to no avail. As the baby's cries became louder and louder, she thought,

"*What will we do?*
Isn't there anyone in this desert to help us?
Are we going to die of thirst in this terrible desert?
I know Allah (SWT) will help us."

She ran back and forth, between the hills seven times but found no water anywhere. Finally, she was so tired that she went back to her baby. As she returned to Ismail, she was surprised to find that he had stopped crying. Even more of a surprise to her was that a stream of fresh, cool water was coming out of the ground right near his feet.

"Water! Water!" cried Hajar. She gave the water to her son and then drank some herself. She then thanked Allah (SWT) for giving them life. She said,

"Thanks to Allah (SWT) who has given us water. How great He is! I knew He would not let us die."

She went into *Sajdah* and thanked Allah (SWT). She was happy Allah (SWT) had saved her and her baby. She piled up sand around the stream to collect the water. This water is called Zamzam. The stream of Zamzam is still running in the same place. It is fresh, healthy and cold water. Muslims from all over the world come to Makkah to visit the Kabah and drink Zamzam.

Lesson 5: The Foundation of Makkah

FOCAL POINT	PERFORMANCE OBJECTIVES	SUGGESTED ACTIVITIES	RESOURCE MATERIAL
A> The growth of Makkah as a city	**The children will:** -learn that Hazrat Hajar's family was the first to settle in Makkah	**The teacher will:** **a.** Read the story of Hajar's joy of finding water, and the settling down of the passing tribe Banu Jerham which resulted in the growth of the holiest city on Earth. (See A below)	The story of Hazrat Hajar's pleasure on finding the water
B> The water attracted travellers and bedouins to settle down and relax	-learn that the presence of water brings people to an area, especially in a desert -know that bedouins live in tents, which are easy to carry and fold.	**a.** Discuss with the children the bedouin lifestyle of early Saudi people (review from Nuh section): -Roaming from place to place in search of food and water. -Herding sheep, goats and camels -Typical diet: dates, honey, meat, goat's milk. The children can bring in food for a Bedouin style snack break, or have a bedouin lunch. **b.** Have the children paint and draw pictures of bedouins and life in the desert	Pictures of tents, goats, sheep, etc. Goat's milk, Honey, Dates, etc. Paint, Paintbrushes, Smocks, etc.
C> The first tribe to settle in Makkah	-learn that the first tribe to settle in Makkah was the tribe of Banu Jerham	**a.** Ask the children comprehension questions: -Why did the birds start coming to the valley? -How did the people of Banu Jerham know about the water in Makkah? -Why did the people of Banu Jerham want to stay in the valley of Makkah? -Why did they ask for Hazrat Hajar's permission to stay in the valley?	
D> The location of Makkah in relation to other cities (Map Skills)	-learn that Makkah was on the crossroads to Syria and Egypt and thus became the center of business commerce	**a.** Explain the kinds of houses that were first built in Makkah (Simple, Adobe/Clay). Show pictures of early Saudi or Yemeni houses and let the children make small house out of clay. (See B below)	Pictures of early adobe houses, Clay
E> SKILLS	VOCABULARY Valley Tent Bedouin Banu Jerham		

FOCAL POINT	PERFORMANCE OBJECTIVES	SUGGESTED ACTIVITIES	RESOURCE MATERIAL
E> SKILLS	VOCABULARY Valley Tent Bedouin Banu Jerham		

THE GROWTH OF THE HOLY CITY

Hazrat Hajar thanked Allah (SWT) for the water. He had provided for her family. She was extremely happy and satisfied with the thought that Allah (SWT) was going to take care of them.

In the desert, water is a precious gift for any living thing. When the thirsty birds spotted the zamzam, they began to come down to the valley to quench their thirst and wash themselves. Soon, Hazrat Hajar had a constant company of birds. She enjoyed this very much.

A few days later, the tribe of Banu Jerham was travelling across the *Hijaz*. The travellers were tired and praying to Allah (SWT) for some shady trees and a spring of water. Suddenly, they spotted all the birds flying towards Makkah. They became overjoyed at the sight, because in the desert, when a lot of birds fly together in a certain direction, it is a sign of water. The tribe followed the birds and to their surprise, found a beautiful woman playing with her baby son. Right next to the two of them was a stream flowing with cool, fresh water.

The head of the tribe came down to Hazrat Hajar and asked her permission to drink the water from the well. She said, "Of course you can drink. This is from Allah (SWT) who has created us and takes care of us." Everyone in the tribe, the men, women, children and animals drank from the well. They all felt better and then started to talk to Hazrat Hajar. The men in the tribe helped to build a small house for Hajar and Ismail.

The Banu Jerham was a noble tribe. They were nice and caring people. They liked the valley of Makkah and wanted to stay there. Hazrat Hajar invited them to make their homes there and live in the valley as her family. Baby Ismail grew up playing with the other children of Banu Jerham. Hazrat Hajar constantly thanked Allah (SWT) for being so kind and giving support to her and the baby.

After a long time, Prophet Ibrahim (A) returned to Makkah to see his wife and son. He was very happy to see the family and the neighbors. He thanked Allah (SWT) for listening to his prayers and providing Hazrat Hajar and Ismail with food, water and good company.

Many travelling tribes would cross through Makkah, and stop there to rest and drink water. Some of the people would decide to stay there and settle down. This way, the valley soon held a small town which became important for trade and business between Yemen and the North.

IQRA' KINDERGARTEN CURRICULUM
ISLAMIC HISTORY
UNIT 5: PROPHET IBRAHIM (A)
Lesson 6: Building the House of Allah (SWT)

FOCAL POINT	PERFORMANCE OBJECTIVES	SUGGESTED ACTIVITIES	RESOURCE MATERIAL
A> The Kabah	The children will: -know that the Kabah is the house of Allah -learn that the Kabah was built by Ibrahim (A) and his son Ismail (A)	The teacher will: **a.** Read to the children the story of building the Kabah. **b.** Talk about the *Kiswa* (the cover of the Kabah) **c.** Using a picture of the Harram, show the location of zamzam in relation to the Kabah. **f.** Talk about the direction of the Kabah from your school or even your classroom. You may use a compass to figure out the Qiblah.	Stories of the Prophets Quran 2: 124 -
B> Muslims face towards the Kabah when they offer Salah	-learn the direction of Qiblah from their classroom.	**a.** If available, use a compass *Musallah* and let the children try to figure out the direction of Kabah. Change the direction of the *Musallah* and discuss the results with the children. Talk about why we face the Kabah while praying. **b.** Talk briefly about Hajj and circulating around the Kabah seven times as Ibrahim (A) did after building the Kabah.	

FOCAL POINT	PERFORMANCE OBJECTIVES	SUGGESTED ACTIVITIES	RESOURCE MATERIAL
C> Father/Son relationship in an Islamic/Human perspective*	-think about their relationships with their fathers.	**a.** Make a chart called "Things I Like to do with My Father" (See A below) **b.** Make a timetable for a week called "Time I Have Spent with My Father." (See B below) **c.** Make a poster called "My father and I" (See C below) **d.** Invite fathers for a Saturday or one day breakfast get-together.	
D> SKILLS Understanding Cooperation Respect Honor Love Obedience to Father	VOCABULARY Qiblah Compass Musallah Kiswa	**a.** Send a progress report home to the parents of the children. (See D below)	

*NOTE TO THE TEACHER: The central theme of this lesson is the relationship between the father and the child. However, in many families, due to special circumstances (ie. illness, death), a child may not be able to spend time with his/her father. In such circumstances the teacher should develop a similar form, dealing with child/mother relationships etc. and encourage participation of the children (some) in the activity. It is important that we remain sensitive to the feelings and needs of every child in the classroom.

THINGS I LIKE TO DO WITH MY FATHER

Procedure:

Write the names of the children on small round stickers and place one in each of the appropriate columns. When completed, count the number of names for each activities are most popular. In the column marked illustration, have the children draw a picture of the respective activity. The teacher should give some directions and examples and then let the children contribute their ideas.

ACTIVITY	ILLUSTRATION	NAMES OF CHILDREN
Going on trips		Ahmed, Nida, Suhail
Going to the movies		Muhammad, Kareem, Khalid
Playing catch		Nabeel, Rasheed, Umar, Fatimah
Reading Quran		Suhail, Khalid, Nida, Fatimah
Praying Salat		Ahmed, Muhammad, Nabeel, Nida
Talking		______, ______, ______

B

TIME I HAVE SPENT WITH MY FATHER (EXAMPLE)

TIME	MONDAY	TUESDAY	WEDNESDAY	THURSDAY	FRIDAY	SATURDAY	SUNDAY
7:00	We ate breakfast		He took me out to				
8:00		He dropped me off at					
9:00						We went jogging	
10:00							
11:00							
12:00					We prayed Friday prayers		He took me to Sunday
1:00							
2:00	He picked me up from school			He picked me up from school			
3:00	We prayed Salah	We read Quran together					He helped me read a book
4:00				We went to visit my aunt		We went to see a movie	
5:00	We ate dinner		We played catch		We went out for dinner		

TIME I HAVE SPENT WITH MY FATHER

TIME	MONDAY	TUESDAY	WEDNESDAY	THURSDAY	FRIDAY	SATURDAY	SUNDAY
7:00							
8:00							
9:00							
10:00							
11:00							
12:00							
1:00							
2:00							
3:00							
4:00							
5:00							

MY FATHER AND I

This is my father. He is _________ tall.
(height)

My father is a/an _________.
(occupation)

I call my father _________.

My father likes to _________.
(activity)

This is me. I am _________ tall.
(height)

I am a _________.
(boy/girl)

He calls me _________.

I like to _________.
(activity)

On the weekends, we like to go to the ________________ together to ________________.
(location) (activity)

We also like to play ________________. The best thing I ever did with my father is________________. I respect my father very much,
(name of a game)

because he is so ________________.

IQRA' KINDERGARTEN CURRICULUM
ISLAMIC HISTORY
Unit 5: Prophet Ibrahim (A)
Lesson 6: Building the House of Allah
Worksheet D: Progress Report

Dear Parents,

Assalam - u - Alaikum

Good Very Good Excellent

That is how I describe the work ____________________ has done on the unit of Prophet Ibrahim (A). Some of the objectives of this unit have been:

1) To help your child develop obedience to the commands of Allah (SWT).
2) To help your child learn about the life of Prophet Ibrahim (A).
3) To familiarize your child with the history of the city of Makkah.
4) To teach your child the direction of Qiblah from his/her school.
5) To develop skills in reading, vocabulary, and oral communication.
6) To develop your child's listening skills.

Thank You for taking the time to read this letter. May the peace and blessings of Allah (SWT) be upon you.

____
Kindergarten Teacher

Appendix

FAVORITE BOOKS FOR KINDERGARTNER'S

Alborough, Jez.	*Esther's Trunk*. Warner, 1989.
Bemelmans, Ludwig.	*Madeline*. Viking Press, 1939.
Bemelmans, Ludwig.	*Madeline's Rescue*.
Bennett, David.	*One Cow Moo Moo*. Holt, 1991.
Blegvad, Erik.	*The Three Little Pigs*. Atheneum, 1980.
Bozzo, Maxine.	*Toby in the Country, Toby in the City*. Greenwillow, 1982.
Brown, Marcia.	*The Three Little Billy Goats Gruff*.
Brown, Margaret Z.	*Goodnight Moon*. Harper, 1947.
Brunhoff, Laurent de.	*Babar's Little Circus Star*. Random House, 1989.
Burton, Virginia L.	*The Little House*. Houghton Mifflin, 1942.
Burton, Virginia L.	*Mike Mulligan and His Steam Shovel*. Houghton Mifflin, 1939.
Calhoun, Mary.	*Cross-country Cat*. Morrow, 1979.
Christelow, Eileen.	*Five Little Monkeys Jumping on the Bed*. Clarion Press, 1990.
Cherry, Lynne.	*Who's Sick Today*? Dutton, 1989.
Cliff, Patricia Rilly.	*Ronald Morgan Goes to Bat*. Viking Press, 1989.
Clifton, Lucille.	*My Friend Jacob*. Dutton, 1980.
Cohen, Miriam.	*Will I Have a Friend*? Macmillan, 1967.
Cole, Joanna.	*It's Too Noisy*! Crowell, 1990.
Conrad, Pam.	*The Tub People*. Harper, Collins, 1990.
Crews, Donald.	*Freight Train*. Greenwillow, 1978.
Crews, Donald.	*Light*. Greenwillow
Daugherty, James H.	*Andy and the Lion*. Viking Press, 1938.
Davis, Jim.	*Garfield's Furry Tales*. Grosset, 1990.
Delton, Judy.	*My Mom Made Me Go To Camp*. Delacorte, 1991.
De Paola, Tomie.	*Charlie Needs a Clock*. Prentice Hall, 1973.

Dinardo, Jeffery. The Wolf Who Cried Boy. Crosset, 1990.

Ehlert, Lois. Fish Eyes: A Book You Can Count On. H.B.J., 1991.

Eyles, Heather. A Zoo in Our House. Warner, 1989.

Flack, Marjorie. Ask Mr. Bear. Macmillan, 1932.

Freeman, Don. Corduroy. Viking Press, 1967.

Goig, Wanda. Millions of Cats. Coward, 1928.

Ginsburg, Mirna. Across the Stream. Greenwillow, 1982.

Ginsburg, Mirna. Good Morning, Chick. Greenwillow, 1980.

Goldone, Paul. The Little Red Hen. Clarion, 1973.

Greene, Carol. Miss Apple's Hats. Milliken, 1990.

Grossman, Bill. The Guy Who Was Five Minutes Late. Harper Collins, 1991.

Hoban, Russell. Bedtime for Frances. Harper, 1960.

Hoban, Russell. Bread and Jam for Frances.

Hoban, Russell. A Babysitter for Frances.

Hoban, Russell. A Birthday for Frances.

Hogrogian, Nonny. One Fine Day. Macmillan, 1971.

Hurd, Edith T. I Dance in My Red Pajamas. Harper, 1982.

Kents, Ezra J. The Snowy Day. Viking Press, 1962.

Kraus, Robert. The Mixed-up Mice Clean House. Warner, 1991.

Lionni, Leo. Frederick. Pantheon, 1966.

Lobel, Arnold. On Market Street. Greenwillow, 1981.

McCloskey, Robert. Make Way for Ducklings. Viking Press, 1941.

McPhail, David. Lost! Joystreet, 1991.

Marshall, James. George and Martha. Houghton, 1972.

Nerlove, Miriam. Just One Tooth. McElderry, 1990

Oppenheim, Joanne. "Not Now!" Said the Cow. Bantam, 1990.

Paresh, Peggy. Good Hunting, Blue Sky. Harper, Collins, 1989.

Paris, Pat. The Frog. Simon & Schuster, 1990.

Polette, Keith. The Winter Duckling. Milliken, 1991.

Potter, Beatrix. Where's Peter Rabbit? Viking Press, 1989.

Rey, Hans A. Curious George. Houghton, 1941.

Ross, Tony. Oscar Got the Blame.

Sendak, Maurice. Where the Wild Things Are. Harper, 1963.

Seuss, Dr. The Cat in the Hat. Random House, 1957.

Slobodkina, Esphyr. Caps for Sale. Addison, 1947.

Spier, Peter. Noah's Ark. Doubleday, 1977.

Steig, William. Sylvester and the Magic Pebble. Windmill, 1969.

Stock, Catherine. A Little Elephant's ABC. Clarion Press, 1989.

Thacher, Hund. Blackberry Rumble. Crown Books, 1991.

Thompson, Carol. Time. Delacorte

Wells, Rosemary. Timothy Goes to School. Dial, 1981.

Wah, Jan. The Adventures of Underwater Dog. Grosset, 1990.

Walsh, Ellen S. Mouse Paint. Harcourt, Brace, Jovanovich, 1990.

Zelinsky, Paul. The Maid and the Mouse and the Odd-shaped House. Dodd, 1981

Zion, Gene. Harry, the Dirty Dog. Harper, 1956.

Zion, Gene. No Roses for Harry. Harper, 1956.

Zion, Gene. Harry By the Sea. Harper, 1956.

Rockwell, Anne. The Three Bears and Fifteen Other Stories. Crowell, 1975.

Thomas, Patricia. "Stand Back" said the Elephant, "I'm Going to Sneeze!", Lothrop, 1991.

RESOURCES FOR KINDERGARTEN TEACHERS

Barron, L.	Mathematics Experiences for the Early Childhood Years. Columbus, Ohio: Charles E. Merril Publishing Co., 1979.
Charlesworth, R., and Radeloff, D.	Experiences in Math for Young Children. Albany, N.Y.: Delmar Publishers, 1978.
DeVires, Rheta and Kohlberg, Lawrence. Children, 1990.	Constructive Early Education: Overview and Comparison with Other Programs. Washington D.C.: Association for the Education of Young
Harns, Christine A.	Child Development. West Publishing Company, 1986.
Harlan, J.D.	Science Experiences for the Early Childhood Years, 2nd ed. Columbus, Ohio: Charles E. Merril Publishing Co., 1980.
Hickman, Jane and Cullinan, Bernice, ed.	Children's Literature in the Classroom. Christopher Gordon Publishing Co., 1989.
Hill, K.	Exploring the Natural World with Young Children. Harcourt, Brace, Jovanovich, 1976.
Kamii, C. and DeVries, R.	Piaget Children and Humben. Washington D.C.: National Association for the Education of Young Children, 1984.
Machado, Jeanne M.	Early Childhood Experiences in Language Arts. Delmar Publishing Co., 1985.
Mayesky, Mary, and Herman, Donald, and Wlodkowski.	Creative Activities for Young Children. Delmar Publishing Co., 1985.
National Geographic Society.	Books for Young Explorers Series. Washington D.C.: National Geographic Society, 1974.
Payne, J.H. Ed.	Mathematics Learning in Early Childhood. Reston, VA: The National Council of Mathematics, 1975.
Scott, L.B. and Garner, J.	Mathematical Experiences for Kindergarten and Primary Teachers. New York: McGraw Hill, 1978.